947
Res

6521

DISCARDED

6521

6521

947   Resnick, Abraham
RES   The Union of Soviet
         Socialist Republics

DATE DUE	BORROWER'S NAME	

02789-1

947   Resnick, Abraham
RES   The Union of Soviet
         Socialist Republics

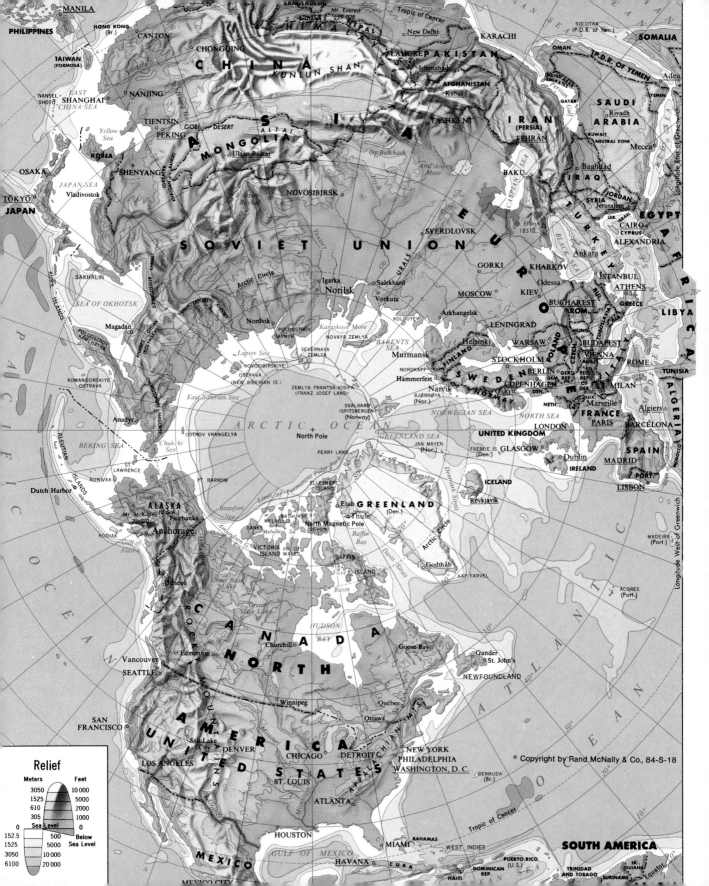

MANILA

PHILIPPINES

HONG KONG (Br.)

CANTON

TAIWAN (FORMOSA)

NANSEI SHOTO

EAST CHINA SEA

SHANGHAI

TIENTSIN
PEKING

KOREA

OSAKA

JAPAN SEA

Vladivostok

TŌKYŌ

JAPAN

CHONGQING

CHINA

KUNLUN SHAN

HIMALAYA

Mt. Everest 29,028

Tropic of Cancer

New Delhi

LAHORE PAKISTAN

Islamabad

AFGHANISTAN

Kabul

KARACHI

SOCOTRA (P.D.R. of Yemen)

SOMALIA

OMAN

P.D.R. OF YEMEN

Aden

YEMEN

SAUDI ARABIA

Riyadh

Mecca

A S I A

GOBI DESERT

MONGOLIA

Ulaan Baatar

SHENYANG

ALTAI

TASHKENT

Oz. Balkhash

IRAN (PERSIA)

TEHRĀN

Baghdad

IRAQ

KUWAIT

NEUTRAL ZONE

UNITED ARAB EMIRATES

QATAR

Persian Gulf

BAKU

SAKHALIN

SEA OF OKHOTSK

Magadan

KOMANDORSKIYE OSTROVA

KAMCHATKA

NOVOSIBIRSK

S O V I E T   U N I O N

Aral'skoye More

CASPIAN SEA

SVERDLOVSK

URALS

GORKI

KHARKOV

MOSCOW

KIEV

Odessa

BLACK SEA

El'brus 18510

TURKEY

Ankara

SYRIA

Jerusalem

ISTANBUL

ATHENS

GREECE

LEBANON ISRAEL

JORDAN

EGYPT

CAIRO

ALEXANDRIA

CYPRUS

LIBYA

E U R O P E

A F R I C A

RED SEA

Longitude East of Greenwich

Arctic Circle

Igarka

Norilsk

Salekhard

Ob'

Yenisey

Vorkuta

Arkhangelsk

LENINGRAD

Helsinki

FINLAND

STOCKHOLM

WARSAW

POLAND

Murmansk

NORDKAPP

Hammerfest

SWEDEN

NORWAY

Oslo

BERLIN

COPENHAGEN

DEN.

BUCHAREST

ROM.

BUDAPEST

VIENNA

AUS.

ROME

MILAN

HUNG.

CZECH.

GER. DEM. REP.

FED. REP. OF GER.

YUGOSLAVIA

BULG.

TUNISIA

ALGERIA

Mediterranean Sea

Algiers

Marseille

FRANCE

PARIS

BARCELONA

SPAIN

MADRID

LISBON

PORT.

Nordvik

Karaskoye More

TAYMYR

SEVERNAYA ZEMLYA

NOVAYA ZEMLYA

BARENTS SEA

NOVOSIBIRSKIYE OSTROVA (NEW SIBERIAN IS.)

ZEMLYA FRANTSA-IOSIFA (FRANZ JOSEF LAND)

Laptev Sea

East Siberian Sea

SVALBARD (SPITSBERGEN) (Norway)

BJØRNØYA (Nor.)

Narvik

NORWEGIAN SEA

NORTH SEA

Anadyr

OSTROV VRANGELYA

Chukchi Sea

BERING SEA

A R C T I C   O C E A N

North Pole

GREENLAND SEA

JAN MAYEN (Nor.)

FAEROE IS. (Den.)

GLASGOW

Dublin

IRELAND

UNITED KINGDOM

LONDON

ST. LAWRENCE

NUNIVAK

Dutch Harbor

ALEUTIAN ISLANDS

ALASKA

Mt. McKinley (U.S.A.) 20,320

Fairbanks

Anchorage

KODIAK

Gulf of Alaska

Yukon

PT. BARROW

Beaufort Sea

Amundsen G.

BANKS

MELVILLE

BATHURST

VICTORIA ISLAND

PR. OF WALES

PEARY LAND

Limit of Permanent Polar Pack

ELLESMERE ISLAND

DEVON

Etah

GREENLAND (Den.)

Thule

North Magnetic Pole

Baffin Bay

BAFFIN ISLAND

Fox Basin

Davis Strait

Godthåb

Denmark Strait

ICELAND

Reykjavik

Arctic Circle

KAP FARVEL

AÇORES (Port.)

MADEIRA (Port.)

Great Bear Lake

Great Slave Lake

Juneau

C A N A D A

ROCKY

Edmonton

Vancouver

SEATTLE

SAN FRANCISCO

N O R T H

HUDSON BAY

Churchill

Winnipeg

Goose Bay

Gander

St. John's

NEWFOUNDLAND

Québec

Ottawa

APPALACHIAN MTS.

NEW YORK

PHILADELPHIA

WASHINGTON, D.C.

A T L A N T I C   O C E A N

40°

50°

30°

Salt Lake City

DENVER

A M E R I C A

U N I T E D   S T A T E S

LOS ANGELES

Missouri

CHICAGO

DETROIT

ST. LOUIS

ATLANTA

HOUSTON

BERMUDA (Br.)

Copyright by Rand McNally & Co., 84-S-18

MEXICO

GULF OF MEXICO

MEXICO CITY

HAVANA

CUBA

MIAMI

BAHAMAS

WEST INDIES

HAITI

DOMINICAN REP.

PUERTO RICO (U.S.)

CARIBBEAN SEA

TRINIDAD AND TOBAGO

FR. GUIANA

SURINAME

SOUTH AMERICA

Tropic of Cancer

Equator

20°

10°

0°

PACIFIC OCEAN

Longitude West of Greenwich

Relief

Meters		Feet
3050		10 000
1525		5000
610		2000
305		1000
Sea Level		0
152.5		500
1525		5000
3050		10 000
6100		20 000

Sea Level

Below Sea Level

0

-5

Enchantment of the World

THE UNION OF SOVIET SOCIALIST REPUBLICS

By Abraham Resnick

Consultants: William G. Rosenberg, Ph.D., Professor of History and Director, Center for Russian Studies, The University of Michigan, Ann Arbor, Michigan

Irwin Weil, Ph.D., Professor of Russian and Russian Literature, Northwestern University, Evanston, Illinois

Edward C. Thaden, Department of History, University of Illinois at Chicago, Illinois

Consultant for Social Studies: Donald W. Nylin, Ph.D., Assistant Superintendent for Instruction, Aurora West Public Schools, Aurora, Illinois

Consultant for Reading: Robert L. Hillerich, Ph.D., Bowling Green State University, Bowling Green, Ohio.

⊄P CHILDRENS PRESS™
CHICAGO

Georgian children with their mothers and grandmother in Tbilisi

For my daughter Janice Resnick Eilen

Library of Congress Cataloging in Publication Data

Resnick, Abraham.
  The Union of Soviet Socialist Republics.

  (Enchantment of the world)
  Summary: An introduction to the geography, history,
economy, government, natural resources, people, and
culture of the world's largest country that covers
almost one sixth of all the land on earth.
  1. Soviet Union—Juvenile literature. [1. Soviet
Union] I. Title. II. Series.
DK17.R44 1984   947   84-7602
ISBN 0-516-02789-1   AACR2

Picture Acknowledgments
Worldwide Photo Specialty, Alexander M. Chabe: Pages
4, 5, 6, 8 (right), 10, 13 (2 photos), 14, 15, 20, 21, (right), 24,
30, 32, 37, 39, 40, 41, 44, 48, 52, 56 (2 photos), 58 (2 photos),
59 (2 photos), 60 (right), 61 (2 photos), 64, 65 (2 photos),
66 (4 photos), 67 (top and middle left), 70 (right), 71, 72, 73
(2 photos), 74 (left), 78 (4 photos), 81, 82 (2 photos), 84 (2
photos), 89, 90, 91 (left), 92, 95 (2 photos), 96, 98, 99, 100
(bottom), 102, 103, 105 (2 photos), 106, 108, 110 (2 photos),
111 (2 photos)
Gladys J. Peterson: Pages 8 (left), 53, 54, 57 (left), 77, 88
Society for Cultural Relations with the USSR: Cover,
pages 19, 21 (left), 27, 33, 35, 43, 57 (right), 62, 67 (middle
right), 75, 86, 100 (top), 107, 113
Root Resources—© Jane H. Kriete: Page 50; © J. William
Langill: Page 60 (left); © Russel A. Kriete: Page 68 (left)
Nawrocki Stock Photo—© Tom Flannigan: Page 55
Hillstrom Stock Photos—© Mary Ann Brockman: Pages 67
(bottom), 68 (right), 69, 70 (left), 74 (right), 91 (right), 104
Robert Harding Picture Library: Page 83
Tass from Sovfoto: 114 (3 photos), 117, 120 (2 photos)
Len Meents: Maps on pages 11 and 50
**Courtesy Flag Research Center, Winchester,
Massachusetts 01890:** Flag on back cover
Cover: May Day celebration in Red Square, Moscow

Mother, child, and grandmother in Leningrad

TABLE OF CONTENTS

Tadzhikstan, with its beautiful natural scenery, is in the southern part of the USSR near the border with Afghanistan.

Chapter 1

LAND OF EXTREMES

The Soviet Union is the largest country in the world. It covers almost one sixth of all the land on earth. It is more than twice the size of the United States. In fact, it is larger than all of North America. The eastern part of the USSR is spread over 40 percent of Asia. The western section is larger than half of Europe.

It is easier to refer to the Union of Soviet Socialist Republics, as many people do, simply as the Soviet Union. Some prefer the name Russia, as it has been called both historically and geographically over the centuries. And just as the United States of America is frequently identified as the USA, the Union of Soviet Socialist Republics is often conveniently labeled the USSR.

Bordering on the USSR are twelve neighbors, plus three oceans, which because of their northern locations are frozen nearly all year. The coastlines of the USSR total more than 30,000 miles (49,500 kilometers), which is more than the distance around the world.

The Soviet Union extends for almost 6,000 miles (9,656 kilometers) from east to west at its greatest distance. From north to south the land stretches for as much as 3,200 miles (5,150 kilometers). These distances are measured along air routes. It would take about twelve hours to fly across the land from east to west. A train ride would require one full week of travel.

From Riga, Latvia, in the extreme northwest, to Vladivostok, in the far southeast, is a distance of 6,800 miles (10,900 kilometers).

Riga, the capital of Latvia (left) and shoppers on Nevsky Prospekt, the main artery in central Leningrad

In 1973-74, fifty-year-old Georgi Bushuyev set out to walk that distance. It took him 238 days to arrive at his destination. According to the *Guinness Book of World Records*, this is a record for long-distance walking in Trans-Asia.

Nearly all of the territory of the Soviet Union lies in the higher northern latitudes. That means that it is situated much closer to the North Pole than to the equator. Leningrad, the USSR's second largest city, is located at a latitude that also crosses the southern tip of Greenland and the southern section of Alaska.

Georgi Bushuyev's journey across the Soviet Union took him through a variety of land regions, different kinds of vegetation zones, large cities, small villages, huge industrial areas, mining regions, and extensive farmlands. The ever-changing landscapes made his long-distance walk interesting and exciting. Day by day he had to adjust his route to cross rivers, bypass lakes, and find paths through thick forests and ways to wade through muddy plains and lowlands.

Climbing the mountains in the west or tramping the rugged plateaus or uplands were tough tests of Bushuyev's physical fitness. The biggest challenge came when he was forced to contend with the enormous snowfields of the grassy plains and even some frozen swamp regions of the Soviet northlands.

Chapter 2

A VAST COUNTRY

The USSR has six main land regions. Georgi Bushuyev walked through five of them en route to Vladivostok. He started his hike in the western region of the Soviet Union called the European Plain, sometimes identified as the Russian lowland.

THE EUROPEAN PLAIN

The European Plain is the home of three fourths of the Soviet people. It has most of the country's industries. The richest soils, including the very productive black earths, can be found there. With Moscow, Leningrad, and Kiev—the nation's three largest cities—located in the region, the European Plain is the center of the Soviet Union's economic life.

For the most part the European Plain is flat, with marshy valleys. Thousands of streams and tributaries run down the low, gently rolling hills of the region. Big, busy rivers drain the low plain. The 2,194-mile (3,531-kilometer) Volga River flows from the Baltic Sea area in the north to empty into the Caspian Sea in the south. It is the longest river in Europe. Other important arteries service the heartland of the country. The winding "3D" rivers, the Dniester, Dnieper, and Don, provide the Russian

*The Dnieper River, the third largest river in Europe, is
at its widest as it flows through Kiev in the Ukraine.*

lowland region with a reliable system for transporting goods and
materials, and with irrigation and hydroelectric power.

In the north the European Plain is wooded. In the south it is
grassy. There the lowland's terrain ends where the Caucasus
Mountains rise dramatically between the Black and Caspian seas.
The Caucasus ranges include volcanic Mount Elbrus (18,481 feet;
5,633 meters), the highest point in Europe.

THE URAL MOUNTAINS

Running north and south at the eastern edge of the European
Plain are the Ural Mountains. This narrow region forms the
boundary between European Russia and Siberia, which is in Asia.
These old mountains have been worn down by streams and wind.
The topsoil has been carried away. Because the Urals are not very
high, they have never protected the country against eastern
invaders. They do, however, have great mineral wealth.

THE WEST SIBERIAN PLAIN

East of the Urals lies the West Siberian Plain. This lowland is the largest level area in the world. It is drained by the Yenisey and Ob rivers. Like many of the Soviet rivers that flow north, they are frozen at their mouths for many months of the year. The relief, or differences in the height of the land from place to place, is so little that rainwater tends to settle on the ground. Many swamp ponds have formed over the land, which is often frozen just below the surface for much of the year. These marshy conditions make the land unsuitable for agriculture, and frequent overflow of the rivers causes flooding and transportation problems.

THE CENTRAL SIBERIAN PLATEAU

The Central Siberian Plateau was the next region encountered by Georgi Bushuyev as he headed eastward. Though the Central·Siberian Plateau has an average height of only 3,000 feet (900 meters), it is deeply cut by streams that flow through ravines and canyons. Lake Baikal, famous for its beauty, is located in the southern part of this region. It is more than 1 mile (1.5 kilometers) deep and is the world's deepest freshwater lake. The Central Siberian Plateau has a wide variety of rich mineral deposits.

THE EAST SIBERIAN UPLANDS

The East Siberian Uplands is the largest region. Much of the area adjoins China to the south. The Pacific Ocean is on the east and the frozen Arctic seas are to the north. This area is usually referred to as the Soviet Far East. Its many mountains are quite high—some ranges rise above 10,000 feet (3,050 meters). Much of the land is wilderness and many kinds of animals roam the forests. The Kamchatka Peninsula extends far into the Pacific Ocean. The scenery there is breathtaking. At the Valley of the Hot Springs rainbow-colored hot-water geysers jet into the air against a backdrop of pink snow. The times of their performances are predictable. As for the twenty-five active volcanoes found on the Kamchatka, however, their eruptions are unpredictable and are much less pleasant to experience.

SOVIET CENTRAL ASIA

Soviet Central Asia, the sixth land region of the Soviet Union, stretches 1,350 miles (2,170 kilometers) to the south of the West Siberian Plain, from the Caspian Sea to the Chinese frontier. Most of the region is low-lying, at or below sea level. The climate is dry, producing extensive deserts. Some parts are sandy, either black or red, while others are rocky or have hard surfaces of baked clay.

In the Soviet Central Asian desert many of the rivers dry up before reaching any body of water. This area is a land of contrasts. An east-west cross section drawing of the region shows the

Vacationers enjoy the mild temperatures in the Black Sea area (left).
Snow-covered village homes on the outskirts of Moscow (right)

Karagiye Depression, 433 feet (132 meters) below sea level, the lowest point in the Soviet Union, as well as the highest point in Russia, Communism Peak (24,590 feet; 7,495 meters) in the Pamirs, a mountain system on the Soviet Union's southern border. Here also is the 44-mile (71-kilometer) Fedchenko Glacier, one of the longest valley glaciers in the world. Its meltwater forms the headstreams of the rivers Surkhan and Amu Darya, the source of water that is now making the USSR's desert lands bloom with cotton plants, sugar beet fields, and flowering gardens.

CLIMATE

The Crimean coast along the northeastern shores of the Black Sea is classified as Mediterranean climate, with mild temperatures, summer drought, and winter rain.

But in most of the USSR winters are particularly long and harsh. Bitter icy winds flow in from the Arctic north. Snow covers more than half the country for six months of the year. Lakes, rivers, and seaports remain frozen for many months. Temperatures fall to extreme lows.

Today, especially in Siberia, buildings are built to keep the heat

13

An alternate means of transportation during the cold, snowy winters

in and the cold out. Often three panes of window glass are used. Walls are extra thick. At least two or three storm doors must be passed through at entrances. Steam heat is piped into the buildings from central generating plants. Construction takes place over four-foot (one-meter) concrete piles to prevent a building from sitting on a foundation of frozen subsurface that could melt and tip the building during the short summer season.

GETTING AROUND IN WINTER

Getting around in the colder parts of the USSR during the winter becomes a seven- or eight-month-long battle. Truck and bus engines must be run every other hour when not in use. Automobiles are often put into hibernation for the winter. Those vehicles that are put to use require four-wheel drive, special batteries, winterized oil, and a double windshield with a sealed air space to prevent frosting and fogging. Boats are lifted onto land or dry docks out of the frozen rivers. Roads have been known to fall apart during the winter. Truck drivers who are brave enough

Removing snow in Red Square, Moscow

sometimes use the deep frozen rivers as their highways. They become reliable routes for transporting winter freight. The transporting of people and goods over railways in the USSR has proven efficient and trains apparently can reach their destinations if track switches are kept from freezing.

The airplane in the Soviet Union takes on a special responsibility, flying above the weather conditions to remote areas that rail lines don't reach. Even so, a unique problem develops for airplanes landing in an extremely cold region. Before passengers are able to leave a cabin, the doors, which become frost-locked aloft, must be defrosted by ground crews using steam jets sprayed from pressure hoses.

WAITING FOR SUMMER

Just as Russian winters are long and cold, so are the winter nights. The more direct rays of the sun are in the Southern Hemisphere during the time of Russian winters. People living in the northern latitudes receive less heat and fewer daylight hours. That is why the people of the Soviet Union look forward to the summer season, as short as it may be.

During the summer months temperatures throughout large portions of the country can become quite warm. Even in the far frontiers of Siberia, cities report thermometer readings that average 60 degrees Fahrenheit (15 degrees Celsius) or more during July. In southern Siberia temperatures can soar into the 90s Fahrenheit (30s Celsius).

SPRING AND AUTUMN

Spring in the Soviet Union is the season of the thaw, bringing mud and flood conditions. Autumn tends to be all too brief and is accompanied by rain showers and sudden drops in temperature. The rain gives way to early snow.

Though the snow remains on the ground for many months of the year throughout large areas of the Soviet Union, much of the land receives very little precipitation at all. The average yearly precipitation—rain, melted snow, and other moisture—in the USSR is considerably less than 20 inches (50 centimeters) a year. Moscow receives rain or snow for about 119 days each year. But in Soviet Central Asia very little precipitation at all is recorded. In the Caucasus, on the other hand, some foothills receive more than 100 inches (250 centimeters) of rain a year.

VEGETATION ZONES

As the climate changes with decreases in latitude across the Soviet Union, from the frigid snowfields of the Arctic Circle to the hot desert regions in the south, the vegetation zones change as well. Five broad east-west belts, each with various kinds of plant life, are found in Europe and Asia. These are the tundra, taiga, steppe, desert, and Mediterranean.

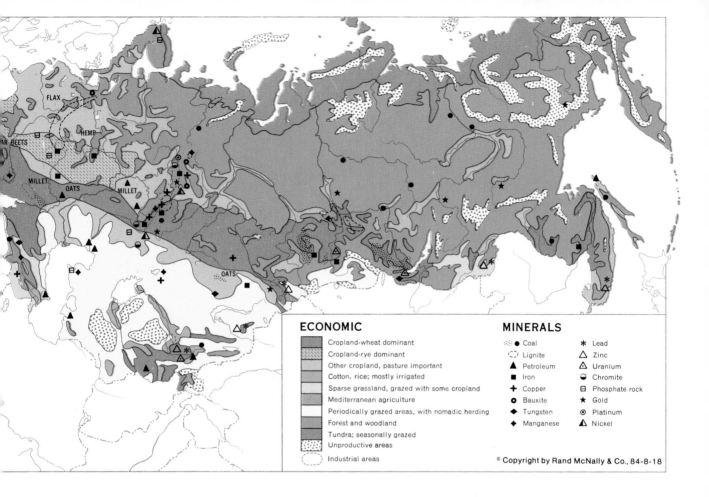

ECONOMIC

- Cropland-wheat dominant
- Cropland-rye dominant
- Other cropland, pasture important
- Cotton, rice; mostly irrigated
- Sparse grassland, grazed with some cropland
- Mediterranean agriculture
- Periodically grazed areas, with nomadic herding
- Forest and woodland
- Tundra; seasonally grazed
- Unproductive areas
- Industrial areas

MINERALS

●	Coal	✳	Lead
◡	Lignite	△	Zinc
▲	Petroleum	△	Uranium
■	Iron	◡	Chromite
+	Copper	⊟	Phosphate rock
○	Bauxite	★	Gold
◆	Tungsten	⊙	Platinum
◆	Manganese	△	Nickel

© Copyright by Rand McNally & Co., 84-8-18

THE TUNDRA

The tundra, a vast treeless plain, is the most northerly
vegetation zone. It extends along the entire Arctic coast and
southward to the first line of trees, or where July temperatures
average 50 degrees Fahrenheit (10 degrees Celsius). It covers over
one seventh of the Soviet Union. The temperatures in the tundra
average far below freezing for nearly nine months of the year.
From September 23 to March 21 the sun never rises above the
horizon. Only small dwarf bushes, wild flowers, and berries grow
during the short summer. Vegetation is mostly moss, peat bogs,
and swamp reeds.

In the winter, Arctic winds pile snowdrifts up to 60 feet (18 meters) high. Agriculture is impossible, but the land supports reindeer and other wild animals. During the summer when the ice thaws, swarms of mosquitoes, so thick they can block out the sun, attack migrating reindeer herds. The mosquitoes get into the nostrils of the large deer, causing great difficulty in breathing. In an attempt to race out of the reach of the mosquitoes, the reindeer panic and stampede. Hundreds can fall dead.

In the tundra zone the ground is frozen all year round, often to a depth of 1,000 feet (305 meters) or more. This permanently frozen subsoil is known as permafrost. It thaws only as deep as 2 feet (.7 meters) below the surface during the brief summer period. A kind of underground glacier exists, and has probably been the same block of solid ice for tens of thousands of years.

THE TAIGA

The taiga, a Russian word meaning "thick forest," begins where the tundra ends. This bank of continuous forest is located in the Soviet subarctic, and for 5,000 miles (8,050 kilometers) spans the width of the USSR, across Europe and Asia. It is estimated that half the area of the Soviet Union is taiga. Apart from birch, aspen, alder, and willow, the trees are all conifers, or cone bearing. Fir, pine, spruce, and larch are dominant. The dense growth of trees in the taiga prevents sunlight from shining through to the forest's floor. This results in low evaporation of rainfall, poor drainage, and spongelike bogs underfoot. It also makes the taiga difficult for humans to tramp through. Animals like the squirrel, lynx, beaver, brown bear, sable, elk, and vole are much more at home there.

Where the trees have been cut down, farm crops such as rye,

Winter in the taiga

oats, and potatoes can be raised. Most of the people who live in the taiga are hunters, fishermen, and lumbermen.

THE STEPPE AND THE DESERT

The third large vegetation zone is the steppe, Russian for "plains." The steppe is a belt of level land south of the taiga. Most of the Soviet Union's best farmland is located in the steppe. It is one of the world's outstanding wheat-growing areas.

When rainfall is plentiful in the Ukraine, the harvests of wheat are great. The Ukraine's famous rich black earth, called *chernozem* in Russian, yields other crops besides wheat. Oats, barley, rye,

Wheat stubble on the steppe

corn, flax, sugar beets, and tobacco are also grown in the western steppe. East of the Ural Mountains, where the rainfall is not as great, the steppe has short grass. This land is better suited for grazing than for farming.

A lack of rainfall affects the region just south of the steppe as well. This is mostly a desert belt, but in some of the northern sections the land is more semidesert. The area is largely inhabited by Uzbek, Kazakh, and other non-Russian groups. The entire area extends eastward from the Caspian Sea. Less than 8 inches (20 centimeters) of rain falls on the land per year, but since it is so hot and dry in the desert, the moisture evaporates quickly.

Scientists are working to develop new strains of cotton (left).
Peach tree in bloom in Armenia (right)

Here cotton, fruits, and vegetables can be grown quite successfully. Many of the rivers in the area are dry beds. But water from the permanent rivers that rise in the faraway mountains can be carried in through irrigation pipes, giving the desert millions of acres of good farmland.

THE MEDITERRANEAN ZONE

The Mediterranean zone on the shores of the Black Sea is the fifth vegetation zone found in the Soviet Union. Compared to the other zones it is quite small. It is called Mediterranean because its climate, landscape, and plants are similar to those in and around the Mediterranean Sea in southern Europe. Citrus fruits are grown. The grapes and olives cultivated here are like those grown in Italy and Greece. Because the warm, dry, sunny weather of the Soviet Mediterranean zone is so inviting, the Black Sea area has become a popular resort.

NATURAL RESOURCES

A great nation must have great natural resources. In addition to its areas of fertile soil, dense timberlands, and many rivers, the USSR has vast mineral resources, both developed and undeveloped. Just about every kind of mineral is found, from aluminum to zinc. Tin is the only important mineral not found in quantities large enough for Soviet needs.

The Soviet Union has about one fifth of the world's coal deposits and considerable reserves of petroleum. The country's natural gas supply is so enormous that it soon may become the world's largest exporter of this energy resource.

Large reserves of iron ore and manganese are found in the Ukraine and the Ural Mountains. The Urals also provide the country with chromium and nickel, two very essential minerals. The republic of Kazakhstan has vast deposits of lead and copper.

Much of the Soviet Union's valuable mineral deposits are found in the far frontier—Siberia, in northern Asia. The name Siberia originally meant "sleeping land." Today Siberia is beginning to awaken. Geologists, like the gold prospectors and fur trappers of the past, are seeking out its hidden treasures. There is an ever-widening interest in mining Siberia's gold, diamonds, and uranium. The oil fields are flowing. The gas is moving to market. Forests and fur products are being transported from Siberia.

Chapter 3

THE FOUNDING OF COMMUNISM

In the seventh century B.C. the Greeks made settlements on the Black Sea coast in Russia. For centuries invaders and settlers crossed the land. Between A.D. 880 and 912 the Russian state was founded at Kiev.

Christianity came to Russia at the end of the tenth century A.D. Because Russia was so isolated, the European Renaissance never spread to it. Until just before World War I, Russia was mainly a country of rich and poor people. The rich upper classes consisted of the tsars and their families, the boyars (noblemen) and their families, and the gentry (landowners or serf owners, but not nobles).

Ordinary people lived miserable lives and had few rights. Serfs were emancipated in 1861 but their lives did not change much. Over the centuries uprisings took place, but none of them was successful. In 1917, a revolution was successful and Tsar Nicholas II abdicated his throne, on March 2, 1917. It soon became clear there was very little government being carried on, little food in the stores, little coal for heating, and little respect for law and order. If Russia was not to lose World War I, something had to be done quickly to stop street demonstrations, desertions from the

БУДУЩЕЕ ЗА КОММУНИЗМОМ!

army, and the growing threat of various revolutionary groups eager to seize power during this crisis. In March a provisional government was organized by the Duma (legislature) under Prince Lvov and Alexander Kerensky. But confusion and conflict remained. People wanted immediate changes.

LENIN AND THE BOLSHEVIKS

The most active of all the political groups that sought to revolutionize Russia at this time was the Bolsheviks, the militant wing of the Russian Social Democratic Labor party. As radicals, they wanted to turn things around right away. They were opposed by the Menshevik wing of the party, who were more moderate in their intentions. The Bolsheviks came under the leadership of Vladimir Lenin, a loyal student of the revolutionary teachings of Karl Marx and Friedrich Engels. Lenin and the Bolsheviks wanted a classless society. They dreamed of the day when no one would be deprived and taken advantage of by the more privileged classes of capitalists and landowners. They wanted a system without large private ownership where some became wealthy at the expense of others. The means of producing goods would be owned by the entire community and all the people would share equally in the work and the goods produced. This idea is known as communism. In 1919 the Bolshevik party was renamed the Communist party.

In 1917 Russia was ripe for revolution. The war continued. Unrest, strikes, and riots jolted Petrograd and other cities. Antigovernment slogans began to appear. Protest rallies became larger and more frequent. People had no patience for the provisional government's talk and debate.

Lenin and his Bolsheviks had something to offer. It was the promise of "peace, land, bread." Lenin vowed that his new order would put an end to the unpopular war and enable the masses to share the land and the fruits of their hard work. He impressed upon them that they would never again be hungry. Follow him, he exclaimed, and they would have "nothing to lose but the chains that bound them." Hundreds of thousands began to follow him.

SOCIAL REVOLUTION

Lenin had a strategy to eventually replace Russian capitalism with Russian communism. But first there would have to be a social upheaval brought on by a revolution of workers leading peasants under the direction and tactics of his Bolshevik political party. In the beginning the working class (proletariat) would have to weaken the influence of the middle class (bourgeois). The bourgeois blocked the working class from gaining higher levels of achievement in the Russian society because it owned the factories and controlled the machines that produced the goods and the

25

profits. Once there was a social revolution it would be easier to get rid of the wealthy ruling class at the top. No longer would there be various classes.

Lenin was a man of action and a natural leader. He could think ahead during a time of crisis and chaos. He knew how to take advantage of a timely opportunity. Lenin saw that by giving authority to the soviets he could seize power for himself and make Russia into a Socialist country. The soviets were the councils (assemblies) chosen to govern provinces and regions. The representatives in the soviets came from the villages and towns. They were not trained politicians. They were selected by factory workers, peasants, and soldiers.

Lenin set out to win the loyalty of the soviets by declaring they should have greater authority to make decisions that would be to their benefit. "All power to the soviets" was his slogan. With their new power, the soviets were told, they could revolutionize and improve all of Russia and make it a great country.

LENIN

Lenin is considered to be one of the most important political figures of the twentieth century. Born in 1870 as Vladimir Ilyich Ulyanov, the son of a school superintendent, he acquired the name Lenin, probably from Russia's great Lena River in Siberia. The city of Simbirsk on the Volga River, in which Lenin was born and educated, was renamed Ulyanovsk after his family name. The city Petrograd (St. Petersburg), where the 1917 armed uprising started, is now known as Leningrad.

When Lenin was seventeen a shocking experience left a deep impression on him. His older brother, a revolutionary, and several

A painting showing peasant messengers visiting Lenin at his headquarters

of his friends planned to assassinate Tsar Alexander III. Their plot was discovered and his brother was executed. Lenin made up his mind to carry on for his brother and become involved in revolutionary work. But first he finished his law studies. While at Kazan University, Lenin was suspended for exciting the students with his open discussion about the need for changes in Russia. Though he worked as a lawyer until 1893, he soon found that he could do more for the "cause" by spreading the socialist views of Karl Marx to the workers. He was arrested and exiled to Siberia for three years. There he began to write in secret about the faults of capitalism. After his release he continued his writing in Switzerland, Germany, and France, calling on the working people to unite into workers' circles to help one another in the struggle for their rights.

In the many leaflets that Lenin smuggled back to Russia, he instructed his "fellow workers" on the need to unite against the oppressors. One such leaflet read: "What are we to do, comrades? To whom are we to look for help? Who is to defend us? We have only ourselves to help and defend us. Taken separately, each of us is nothing, but all of us together repesent a great force. So may everyone unite with his comrades in the fight for the righteous cause, for a better life."

"DOWN WITH WAR"

Lenin lived abroad for ten years. But he played a major role in directing the Bolsheviks in the preparation of the socialist revolution. As World War I dragged on and the Germans advanced toward Petrograd, the morale of the Russian troops reached a new low. They were tired of fighting a war for which they had little enthusiasm. The Bolsheviks were becoming very popular with their cries of "Down with war." The Kerensky government and its bourgeois supporters seemed to be doing nothing. The Bolsheviks encouraged the soldiers to go home. Thousands did. The government started to go into a decline.

When Lenin received word of the events taking place in Russia, he decided to return home and take personal charge of the revolution. He arrived by train from Finland in April, 1917, and was welcomed at the Petrograd station by a huge crowd of cheering supporters. Lenin turned the Bolsheviks on a radical course designed to seize power. In July, Bolshevik soldiers led an armed demonstration known as the July Days. The Bolsheviks were accused of treason and Leon Trotsky, one of their leaders, was arrested. Lenin went into hiding.

In September Lenin again returned and began plans for the revolution. When he learned he was about to be arrested for his activities, he went into hiding on a farm at the Finnish border. There he continued to direct the preparations, especially the organization of the Red Guards, the most loyal of his revolutionary detachments.

THE REVOLUTION

The flag of the revolutionaries was raised over the palace of the tsars on October 26, 1917. The Bolsheviks called it the "victory of socialism." The revolution actually took place on October 25, 1917, according to the Russian calendar used at that time. That is why it is often referred to as the October Revolution by the Russians. According to the Western calendar the day was November 7.

Lenin, working closely with Leon Trotsky and other comrades, planned their coup. It involved storming the Winter Palace and capturing members of the Kerensky provisional government. The drawbridges, the telegraph office, the telephone exchange, railway stations, and power plants were to be taken by surprise in quick bold moves. This would cut off the palace headquarters from the rest of the country. No troops could be called up since it would be impossible to send orders to army garrisons outside Petrograd. In the meantime, the Petrograd garrisons had become "Bolshevized," and were in sympathy with Lenin, Trotsky, and other rebel leaders. They could be counted on to back the revolutionaries.

The coup went according to plan. At 9:40 P.M. the Russian cruiser *Aurora* fired the shot that signaled the rebel charge to the gates of the Winter Palace. The Bolshevik Red Guards drew first

The cruiser Aurora, *whose shot signaled the rebel charge, is permanently docked in the Neva River in Leningrad.*

blood. The great October Revolution was underway. Masses of armed workers, peasants, and former soldiers swept past the palace fortifications. The fight was very fierce, penetrating into the palace itself. Government officers resisted, firing from the top of stairs and from behind columns and marble statues. At 2:10 A.M. the rebels broke into the room where the frightened ministers and other government officials were hiding. They were immediately arrested. The revolution was realized. It took little time for the Bolshevik rule to extend to Moscow and the rest of Russia.

THE NEW BOLSHEVIK GOVERNMENT

A newly written Soviet constitution appeared on July 10, 1918. It provided for new laws and many radical changes. Much of the country's privately owned industries, banks, mines, land, and property was put under the ownership or control of the national government. Foreign trade was also nationalized. Workers were required to work only eight hours a day, but unemployment was severe. All of the church's political power and most of its property were taken over by the government. Prices were controlled. National groups and minorities were granted rights they had not had before. Education was now to be free. A Red Army was formed and all men were to receive military training. Women were proclaimed, in the eyes of the law, equal to men.

The new Russian leaders had to make good on the promise to make peace with Germany. The Germans knew that the Bolsheviks were unable to fight against them at the same time they were fighting enemies on their home front. They offered the Russians a one-sided peace treaty by which the whole of the Ukraine was lost to Russia. Lenin, knowing that he would have to give his total attention to domestic matters to keep his rule, agreed to the terms of the Treaty of Brest-Litovsk, ending Russia's involvement in World War I.

CIVIL WAR

But the Brest-Litovsk treaty did not bring peace to Russia. The transition from one form of government to another did not go smoothly. The people and political parties that would stand to lose the most fought back at the Communists, as they were beginning to be identified in 1918. The bitter feeling of the counterrevolutionaries, the group out of power that opposed the Communists, got out of hand. The hatred between the groups soon grew into a bloody civil war. Russians were pitted against Russians—Communists, called "Reds," against former officials, nobles, bourgeois, gentry, military men, and clergy, called "Whites."

The brutal civil war lasted for more than three years. Battles were fought on many fronts from Siberia to Poland. White forces were mustered throughout Russia, from the Crimea in the far south to Arkhangelsk in the far north. As the war progressed the

In May 1919 Lenin speaks to new troops in Red Square.

Red Army grew to over five million men. Terror, famine, and sickness swept over the land. Roaming destructive bands relied on might over right. There was a tremendous amount of drinking and lawlessness. Suspicion had no limitations. Firing squads were kept busy. Thousands upon thousands of children were orphaned. Families were separated. People resorted to living in railroad box cars and railway stations for months on end. Men, women, and children were forced to work in labor camps and mines. Chaos replaced any likeness of normal living.

Fearing the rapidly rising power and worldwide spread of the "Red Menace," a number of foreign countries sent troops to support the White armies and try to smother the Red forces. British, Japanese, French, and American army detachments were sent to Russia to help the Whites march on Moscow. Even the Poles, a traditional foe of the Russians, became involved on the side of the counterrevolutionaries. Fifty thousand Czechs joined in the fight against the Communists in Siberia, thousands of miles from home.

Lenin addressing the Second All-Russian Congress of Soviets

A NEW START

By 1921 the war had ended. The White armies gave up their struggle. Foreign armies left Russian soil. But the price paid for victory was very high. Millions of people had been killed. Perhaps as many as 7,000,000 died from hunger and epidemics in the first two-and-one-half years of Soviet rule. The country was in ruins. When a number of foreign churches, nations, and other humanitarian groups learned about the horrible conditions and suffering of the Russians, they were quick to forgive and forget their politics. Food, relief aid, and tons of supplies were sent to Russia, along with experts from many different fields to help the Russian people get off to a new start.

The fledgling Communist government had survived.

Chapter 4

THE GROWTH OF THE USSR

THE STALIN YEARS

In 1924 Lenin died of natural causes, although he still carried an assassin's bullet in his body. In the decades following his death many other Communist leaders also died, but of unnatural causes—they were executed. There were many purges. The man who gained control of the Communist party, Joseph Stalin, was responsible for most of them. In a bitter struggle for power Stalin charged those Communist leaders who disagreed with him with betraying the new ideals. Hundreds were brought to trial, were usually found guilty and then faced the firing squads. Even Leon Trotsky, one of the top Bolshevik pioneers, was exiled and fled to Mexico, where he was followed and assassinated.

THE IRON CURTAIN

Joseph Stalin hoped for an eventual collapse of the capitalistic forces in the West. He also feared that these same forces would try to prevent communism from succeeding in the USSR. Suspicious of other leaders and other countries, he began to draw a curtain

After Lenin died in 1924, a number of powerful men vied for power. By 1927 Joseph Stalin was in power and he ruled until his death in 1953.

around the Soviet Union. After World War II that curtain became an "iron curtain." It took the form of a wall of steel armaments to protect the country from unfriendly foreigners. The ring of armed military might was also used to prevent Russians from leaving their homeland without permission. And the curtain prevented outsiders from seeing what was going on inside Russia.

JOSEPH STALIN

Inside Russia at this time Stalin began to live up to his name. Stalin, which means "man of steel," was a name he had selected. He was born in Georgia, a province in southern Russia, with the family name of Dzhugashvili. Stalin was as hard and unbending as the wall of steel he built around the Soviet Union. He ruled his country with force and terrorism. He had complete power. His word was obeyed for more than a quarter of a century until he died in 1953. His strict policies became known as Stalinism.

Joseph Stalin faced many problems in trying to introduce "socialism" in the Soviet Union. When his plans failed, or were slow to get results, he was quick to blame others. Stalin was able to round up many scapegoats. They were often brought before courts on charges of sabotage. The punishment for sabotage during the Stalin era was suspension from the Communist party, loss of a job, and a sentence of hard labor in Siberia. Millions of innocent men and women were exiled for crimes they never committed.

THE CHANGEOVER

During the early years of the changeover to a socialist type of government, many farmers and peasants were also sent away for refusing to cooperate. When they heard the government was about to seize their lands and animals, they quickly slaughtered the livestock and offered the meat for sale. This brought about a desperate food shortage. The villagers who owned small plots of land didn't want their holdings to be organized into large government-owned collective farms.

FIVE-YEAR PLANS

In 1929 Stalin started the first of a series of five-year plans to improve the country. These plans were set up to modernize Soviet agriculture and to build new mills, factories, mines, and power

A poster in Moscow reads, "We will build communism; we will live under communism."

stations. Transportation was to be improved. Living standards were to be raised. New cities were to be built, with thousands upon thousands of apartment blocks. The army was to be made stronger. Education was to be extended to all citizens—for the first time millions of people would be taught how to read and write. Better health services and more doctors would be provided to care for everyone—free of charge.

Great demands were put on the people to work hard to produce the amount of goods and services called for in each of the five-year plans. Those who did their fair share were rewarded with ration coupons to buy things they needed, including food. "He who does not work shall not eat" was a slogan often used to spur the workers to produce their quotas. Those who turned out more than the goals set for them were praised and honored. They were known as "Stakhanovites." Alexei Stakhanov was a miner who dug a record-breaking 102 tons (93 metric tons) of coal in one six-hour shift. He was held up as a national hero, a prime example of the great effort and sacrifice needed to make the new Soviet plans successful.

Most of the plans' objectives were reached, but problems remained over the years in producing enough food and housing for all. Perhaps greater progress could have been made had it not been for the urgent need to set aside one fourth of the national income for a military buildup. By 1933 frightening events were beginning to take place in Germany. Adolf Hitler was a ruthless dictator bent on taking over all of Europe. Hitler's Nazi party had gained control of Germany. Because of Hitler's growing war machine, Stalin determined to make new changes and new plans. He realized that he would have to prepare for war.

WORLD WAR II

World War II, which the Soviets often call the Great Patriotic War, began in the east in September, 1939, when both Germany and the USSR invaded Poland. In June, 1941, Hitler ordered his armies to invade Russia. The German generals thought that a victory over the Soviet armed forces would be quick and easy. Hitler's intelligence agents predicted that Russian citizens, unhappy with communism, would welcome German troops on their soil. It didn't turn out that way.

Stalin took over leadership of the war effort. He named himself premier, marshal, generalissimo, and supreme commander in chief of the Soviet armed forces. As a leader he showed great skill and stubborn courage. The Red Army and Soviet civilians rallied behind their leader and fought the Germans with a tremendous show of patriotism and bravery under fire.

The Nazis threw their military might at the Russians at three

In 1942, during the siege of Leningrad, trucks crossed the "Road of Life" on Lake Ladoga bringing supplies, food, and medicine.

points: Leningrad, Moscow, and the coal- and goods-producing regions of the south. Apparently the Nazi generals forgot about the failure of Napoleon's armies in Russia more than a century before.

The fighting between the Russians and Germans was extremely fierce. The Nazis stormed Leningrad with a large force of their best troops. They bombed and shelled the city for nine hundred days. The city was almost surrounded and cut off from the rest of the country. Food and fuel were scarce; there was no water, electricity, or transportation. The few supplies that reached Leningrad were trucked over frozen Lake Ladoga, which is east of Leningrad, in winter. In summer barges delivered supplies. Thousands of citizens died of wounds, illness, and starvation. The inhabitants of Leningrad worked twice as long and much harder than usual. In the winter of 1942-43 Russian engineers laid a railroad track over the frozen surface of Lake Ladoga and freight cars were able to bring in food, fuel, and ammunition. Finally in 1944 the siege was lifted and the city was saved from total ruin.

Many other cities came under Nazi attacks. Sevastopal in the Crimea was bombarded for eight months before it was evacuated.

German planes flying over Leningrad in September 1941

The main attempt to take Moscow was slowed down at Smolensk. The Germans, even after three months of fighting, failed to enter Moscow. At Stalingrad, which was renamed Volgograd in 1961, the Nazis launched a tremendous offensive to capture the lower Volga area and the Caucasus. They hoped to cut off food and fuel coming from the south. Then with the fall of Stalingrad the bulk of the German army could move up the Volga River and attack Moscow from the rear. It never happened.

THE VICTORIOUS RED ARMY

In what turned out to be the bloodiest battle of the war the Russians took the brunt of the German onslaught. For forty-seven days Stalingrad was bombed daily by one thousand planes and cannon. The city was a battlefield for five months. There was house-to-house fighting. With their backs to the river, the Russian troops stood firm. Then they counterattacked. An entire German army of 330,000 men was captured or destroyed. The famous battle of Stalingrad was the turning point of the war. Soon it was

Still holding out, Soviet guns in Leningrad fire on the Germans in January 1944.

the German army that was retreating. The Red Army forced it all the way back to Berlin, where the Nazis surrendered in 1945.

The war against Hitler caused suffering and destruction beyond imagination. Cities, towns, and villages were torn apart, razed, and virtually wiped from the face of the earth. The Russian losses were staggering. Over twenty million were killed or missing. At least one Russian in ten died during the war. Many of the dead were women, children, and old people. Millions more were wounded. Twenty-five million Russians were without homes after the war.

DIVISION OF GERMANY

The Soviet Union did not shoulder the weight of the war against Germany alone. England and the United States were deeply involved in the fight against the Nazis on the western front. The United States sent the Soviet Union considerable amounts of military supplies and food. The president of the United States, Franklin D. Roosevelt, and the prime minister of Great Britain, Winston Churchill, met secretly with Stalin to plan a combined war effort. Informal arrangements were made to allow eastern Europe to be in the Soviet sphere of influence. Decisions were also made about the control of territories and occupied countries. Germany was to be divided into four parts and weakened to the point of never being able to wage war again.

THE COLD WAR

In the years following the war the Soviet Union entered a period that came to be known as the "cold war." On one side of the iron curtain, especially in eastern Europe, Soviet military power established Stalinist governments. On the other side of the iron curtain the United States, Canada, and a number of western European countries formed the North Atlantic Treaty Organization (NATO), which was designed to try to stop the spread of communism. The two sides faced each other on many issues and in many places without breaking diplomatic relations.

THE BERLIN WALL

In 1948 the Communists tried to expand their influence in key locations in Europe. They wanted to see how far they could go before the West would resist their moves. They put a land blockade around Berlin, the former capital of Germany, which after the war had been divided into American, Soviet, British, and French sectors. The United States immediately began an airlift to Berlin, flying hundreds of tons of supplies to the city. The blockade was broken by this very effective, but embarrassing, maneuver. The Soviets were embarrassed again when so many Germans fled to the West that, in 1961, East Germany, the Communist ally of the USSR, had to build a wall to stop them.

*Yuri Gagarin,
the first person
to orbit the earth*

NIKITA KHRUSHCHEV

Shortly after Stalin's death in 1953 Nikita Khrushchev came to power in the Soviet Union. He denounced Stalin for massive crimes against the people and freed political prisoners. But in 1956, when some of the citizens of Communist Hungary rebelled against their government, Soviet tanks were sent in to crush the revolt. Thousands of Hungarians also fled to the West.

SPUTNIK

In 1957 the Soviet Union surprised the world with a great scientific achievement—the launching of *Sputnik*, the first space satellite. In 1961, Yuri Gagarin became the first person to orbit the earth. For a time the Soviets led in a new kind of competition between East and West—the space race.

LEONID BREZHNEV

In 1964 Khrushchev was removed from high office. Eventually Leonid Brezhnev took charge of running the country. In 1968

*Leonid Brezhnev succeeded
Nikita Khrushchev as head
of the Communist party
and ruled until his
death in 1982.*

Soviet troops invaded Communist Czechoslovakia to end Czech attempts to introduce economic and democratic changes that Moscow considered dangerous.

Over the years trade and diplomatic relations between the East and West have been affected by the foreign policies of the United States and the Soviet Union. The Soviets helped train and supply the forces that fought against the United States in Vietnam during the 1960s and 1970s. In the late 1960s a long-standing feud between the Soviet Union and the People's Republic of China broke into open hostilities on the Siberian border.

When the USSR sent troops into Afghanistan in 1979, the United States refused to send grain shipments to the Soviets. The Americans also boycotted the 1980 Olympic games held in Moscow. On the other hand, the huge Soviet pipeline built to bring Siberian natural gas to western Europe in the 1980s was financed and supplied in part by Western technology.

YURI ANDROPOV

Leonid Brezhnev died in November, 1982. He was succeeded by Yuri V. Andropov, the former leader of the K.G.B., the Communist secret police. In 1984 Andropov died and was succeeded by Konstantin Chernenko.

Chapter 5

THE GOVERNMENT

THE COMMUNIST PARTY

In the Soviet Union the constitution allows only one political party to exist. The Communist party of the Soviet Union (CPSU) is the "leading and guiding force of Soviet society." It has full control over the government, the armed forces, trade unions, the press, schools, and all large organizations.

The Communist party of the Soviet Union is like a large corporation. A small group of leaders makes the important decisions for the party and directs the operations of the government at home and abroad. The party bosses plan a program that becomes the "party line." The program is then put into the government machinery, to be carried out down through the ranks of lesser officials.

The Communist party is a select organization. Only about 6 percent (about 16 million) of all Soviet citizens belong to it. It is kept small in order to keep discipline and rigid control. The members have great influence wherever they work. Membership can give them special privileges.

The organization of the party is like a huge pyramid. At the broad base of the structure are more than 320,000 primary organizations, with from three to three hundred members in each unit. The foundation for the pyramid is formed at places of employment. Each local unit elects delegates to confer with higher party groups in other towns and plants, which in turn elect a higher level of delegates to the district party group. Moving upward on the pyramid, district delegates are then elected to a provincial party group, then to a republic's party group, and finally to the All-Union Party Congress, the highest organization in the Communist party.

THE POLITBURO

The All-Union Party Congress has about five thousand delegates from the fifteen republics of the Soviet Union, together with men and women chosen from the autonomous republics, regional areas, and representatives from Communist parties around the world. The congress is supposed to meet at least every five years, but it rarely does. Its four-hundred-member Central Committee meets twice a year. A Politburo (Political Bureau) and a Secretariat, selected by the party leaders, is formed to act for the party during the long periods when the All-Union Party Congress is not in session.

The Politburo is the real center of power in the party and therefore has the most authority in the government. It sets all the major Soviet policies and programs, both national and international. About twelve regular voting members and seven nonvoting alternate members meet in secret so as not to reveal their positions on the issues discussed. Politburo members hold the most influential jobs as heads of the various ministries of the

THE COMMUNIST PARTY
Only one political party exists in the USSR. It has full control over the government, the armed forces, trade unions, the press, education, and all large organizations. About 6 percent of the Soviet citizens belong to the Communist party.

THE CENTRAL COMMITTEE
This four-hundred-member committee meets twice a year and selects the members of the Politburo and Secretariat. The general secretary of the Central Committee heads the Politburo and Secretariat and is the most powerful person in the USSR.

THE POLITBURO OF THE CENTRAL COMMITTEE	THE SECRETARIAT OF THE CENTRAL COMMITTEE
The Politburo sets all of the major Soviet policies and programs, both national and international. There are about twelve regular voting members and seven nonvoting alternate members who meet in secret. Whatever they decide should happen is what happens in the Soviet Union. The Politburo power cannot be disputed.	The ten-member administrative staff of the Central Committee runs the day-to-day affairs of the USSR and makes certain party policies are carried out according to the chain of command.

government. Whatever they decide should happen is what happens in the Soviet Union. The cannot be disputed, nor can their powers be checked or balanced.

THE SECRETARIAT

Assisting the Politburo is the Secretariat, a ten-member administrative staff of the Central Committee. It makes certain that party policies are carried out according to the chain of command, right down to the local bureaucracies of the Communist party. The general secretary of the Central Committee is in charge of both the Secretariat and the Politburo. This is the most powerful position in the Soviet Union. The Secretariat's staff of one thousand professional party secretaries exerts great

The party delegates meet in the Palace of Congresses inside the Kremlin in Moscow. Completed in 1961, it is built of white marble.

influence over Soviet life on a daily basis. The party secretaries are the main gears in the Communist apparatus.

THE FRAMEWORK OF GOVERNMENT

The framework of the Soviet federal government is also designed like a pyramid. The lower bodies of government are responsible to the levels of government above it. At the top is the Supreme Soviet of the USSR, a two-house parliament. Each house has about 750 members, called deputies. They are elected to five-year terms and are expected to pass all laws proposed by the Communist leaders. Voters have little choice but to vote for a single hand-picked candidate.

The Soviet of the Union has one deputy to represent each district of about 300,000 persons. In the Soviet of Nationalities each of the fifteen union republics is represented by 32 deputies. Other regions within the republics elect the rest of the 750 members. The Supreme Soviet "elects" the members of its Presidium (legislative body) and the Council of Ministers (a cabinet). The chairman of the Presidium is considered to be the head of state of the Soviet Union. The Council of Ministers is the most important executive body of the government. The chairman of the Council of Ministers is the government's chief executive and is usually referred to as premier or prime minister.

The local governments fall under the administration of the fifteen union republics and the twenty autonomous republics. Each has a constitution and a supreme soviet with a presidium and a council of ministers. The lower levels of government have soviets (councils) of people's deputies. Most of these councils elect executive committees to take care of local matters.

THE COURT SYSTEM

The Soviet court system is guided by the policies of the Communist party. The chief legal officer of the country is elected by Communist party leaders and appointed by the Supreme Soviet to a five-year term. He is known as the procurator-general and functions like an attorney general. Judges throughout the land are also elected to five-year terms. The courts range from local people's courts to regional courts. Each republic has a supreme court and there is a supreme court of the USSR, the highest court of the country.

In the Soviet Union one can be brought to trial for speaking against the Soviet political and social system, if it is done with intent to weaken the power of the state. Also, in the Soviet Union there is a special category of crime for someone who neglects or takes advantage of an official position in a state business. It is forbidden to "speculate," to buy and resell a product for personal profit. The maximum term in prison is fifteen years, but the death penalty exists for certain types of crimes, such as embezzlement of state property. Soviet convicts are likely to serve full terms without parole. While in prison or in a work camp, repeated offenders or dangerous criminals are forced to do hard labor.

A view of Moscow, the capital city of the Soviet Union

LITHUANIA
Vilnius

LATVIA
Riga

ESTONIA
Tallinn

BYELORUSSIA
Minsk

Kiev

MOLDAVIA
Kishinev

THE UKRAINE

Moscow

GEORGIA
Tbilisi

ARMENIA
Yerevan

AZERBAIDZHAN

Baku

RUSSIAN SOVIET FEDERATED SOCIALIST REPUBLIC

Ashkhabad

KAZAKHSTAN

UZBEKISTAN

Tashkent

Alma-Ata

TURKMENIA

Frunze
KIRGHIZIA

Dushanbe
TADZHIKSTAN

Chapter 6

THE FIFTEEN REPUBLICS

The Soviet Union is divided into fifteen union republics. Each of these land divisions has a predominant ethnic group living within its boundaries. The Russian Soviet Federated Socialist Republic (RSFSR) is about 550 times greater in area than the smallest republic, the Armenian Soviet Socialist Republic (ASSR). Each union republic has its own government to run local affairs, but control of major matters stems from Moscow, the national capital.

RUSSIAN SOVIET FEDERATED SOCIALIST REPUBLIC

The Russian Soviet Federated Socialist Republic spans two continents—Europe and Asia. It is first in economic might, cultural development, and population. More than half of the citizens of the USSR live in this republic. Its industrial production is tremendous, with factories turning out everything from minute instruments to monstrous nuclear icebreakers. The world's biggest hydroelectric power stations have been built in the republic. Thousands of miles of pipelines and railways, along with a great river and canal system, transport oil, gas, minerals, timber, and other valuable resources from places of origin to refineries, mills,

Kiev, the capital of the Ukraine, lies on both sides of the Dnieper River.

and factories all over the vast country. Siberia and the Soviet Far East regions are located within the RSFSR.

THE UKRAINE

The Ukraine is another highly developed region. The Ukrainian republic is situated in the southwest and is about as large as France. It was here that the Eastern Slavic state, Kievan Rus, began. Today, its capital, Kiev, is one of the most beautiful cities in the country. There is an old Russian proverb that says "Moscow is the heart of Russia, St. Petersburg (now Leningrad) its head, but Kiev is its mother." Not only is the Ukraine important for its iron ore, coal, heavy industry, and manufacturing, but it is also referred to as the "breadbasket" of the Soviet Union. Its warm climate and fertile soil help to produce high yields of sugar beets,

A vineyard in Moldavia

wheat, and other agricultural products. Many scientific institutes and laboratories are found in the republic.

THE MOLDAVIAN REPUBLIC

The Moldavian republic covers 13,000 square miles (33,700 square kilometers). It occupies only one tenth of one percent of the country. It is sandwiched between the Ukraine and Romania. Many of its people speak a Romance language similar to Romanian or Italian. The region was once ruled by the Turks and conquered by the Romans. The Moldavian people love good food and good music. The food industry has always been a major source of its income. The republic produces fine grades of wine, canned fruits, and vegetables. Moldavian folk music is enjoyed throughout the USSR and Europe.

Since most of Minsk was destroyed during World War II, many sections are new.

BYELORUSSIA

Byelorussia, known as "White Russia," has experienced great changes since World War II. As the westernmost republic, with its low-lying southern marshlands, it was on the highway of war for armies pushing eastward toward Moscow and Leningrad. In Minsk, the large capital city, as well as in smaller towns, the wartime suffering was staggering. Every fourth person in the republic was killed. A large Jewish population that lived in Minsk and the surrounding villages was wiped out. Though the republic was at one time one of the poorest regions of European Russia, rapid growth now is taking place. Minsk has become the center of a thriving machine tool and motor vehicle manufacturing industry. Byelorussia, like the Ukraine, holds a separate membership in the United Nations.

The old town section of Tallinn has well-preserved medieval architecture.

SOVIET BALTIC REPUBLICS

The Soviet Baltic republics of Lithuania, Latvia, and Estonia have much in common. Each lies on a gulf along the eastern coast of the Baltic Sea. Riga, the capital of Latvia, and Tallinn, the capital of Estonia, are both large port cities. Vilnius, the capital of Lithuania, is an important trading hub about 125 miles (200 kilometers) northwest of Minsk. The people have strong national ties to their pasts, which go back to medieval times. Their industries, natural resources, and architecture are quite similar, too. These republics, known as the "Soviet West," have the highest standard of living in the USSR. Some nations refuse to recognize these "three sisters" as part of the USSR.

THE TRANSCAUCASIAN REPUBLICS

As the Baltic republics are influenced by the sea, the three Transcaucasian republics of Azerbaidzhan, Armenia, and Georgia

Lake Ritsa lies in the forests and meadows of the Caucasus Mountains (left). Yerevan, the capital of Armenia (right)

are affected by mountains. They all lie in the southern part of the USSR between the Black and the Caspian seas. Historically this area has been a meeting place for Eastern and Western peoples as well as a land route for countless invaders of bygone centuries.

Sunny Armenia is the oldest nation in the Soviet Union. Her people have suffered much from ruthless conquerors, yet the great national pride and rich culture of a very talented nationality lives on. Armenians have a very strong will. The emblem of Armenia shows wheat and grapes, two major agricultural products of the republic. Many kinds of machines, textiles, and chemicals are produced in factories. Most noticeable of all on the Armenian emblem is a picture of Mount Ararat, where some believe Noah's ark may have landed after the Great Flood of biblical times. But now this cherished mountain is part of Turkey, a cause of considerable unhappiness for all Armenians.

Azerbaidzhan has long been a major oil producer. Cotton also dominates its economy. It is not surprising that Azerbaidzhan's

A grandmother is called a babushka *(left).*
Oil and gas are transported through pipelines (right).

state emblem is marked by an oil derrick and cotton balls. Much
of the machinery used in the USSR's oil processing industry is
made here as well. The fruit grown in the region is exceptional.
The republic claims to have more centenarians than any other
area of the world. It is said that the oldest man in the world
during this century, Medjid Agayev, celebrated his one-hundred-
and-forty-second birthday there in 1977.

Georgia is rich in mineral deposits, especially manganese ore.
The republic produces steel, metal, automobiles, locomotives,
computers, fertilizers, and fabrics. Georgia accounts for most of
the country's output of tea and citrus fruit. Her people are superb
craftsmen in the art of metalwork, and have been for centuries.

A number of present-day Georgians live long lives as well. At
least one in every 2,500 is one hundred years old or older.
Millions of people vacation each year at Georgia's popular resorts.
On land they enjoy health spas, at the sea they sun themselves at
the many beaches, and at higher altitudes they hike or ski in the
magnificent mountains of the Georgia republic.

Leading the family camels home from pasture in Turkmenia (left)
Kazakhs enjoy eating roasted lamb on skewers (right).

REPUBLICS EAST OF THE CASPIAN SEA

East of the Caspian Sea lie five fascinating republics:
Kazakhstan, Kirghizia, Turkmenia, Uzbekistan, and Tadzhikstan.
To understand the background of their residents today, it is
important to realize that many of their parents or grandparents
were horse-riding nomads roaming across steppe meadows, or up
and down mountain slopes. One hundred years ago most of the
inhabitants of the dry plains and desertlike terrains of central Asia
were herdsmen or oases farmers.

The Kazakh republic is the second largest republic in the Soviet
Union. It extends from the Caspian Sea to China. Since *stan* means
"country," the people who live in Kazakhstan live in the "country
of the Kazakhs." Its capital city is Alma-Ata. Today Kazakhstan
has more than 25,000 industrial enterprises. It is one of the Soviet
Union's main suppliers of coal. Agriculture, grain growing in
particular, is now possible in Kazakhstan since a canal was built
to bring waters from Siberian rivers into the region.

Mountain climber in the Tien-Shan Mountains,
(left) and girls from Ashkhabad, Turkmenia

Kazakhstan is the site of the Baikonur cosmodrome from which all Soviet satellites and spaceships are launched. In 1982 two Soviet cosmonauts returned to earth in Kazakhstan after setting a record of 211 days in orbit.

There are more sunny days in Kirghizia than anywhere else in the USSR. The climate is ideal for growing grapes, cotton, apricots, and tobacco. But since water is scarce in Kirghizia, the breeding of fine-fleeced sheep and pedigreed horses is more important than growing crops.

Turkmenia is a unique land full of contrasts. Its capital, Ashkhabad, is a good-sized city, but in vast reaches of the interior hardly anyone lives for hundreds of miles around. The republic blends the ancient with the modern. Some people ride on horses, others ride in buses. Some live in tents, others in apartments. Some are weavers of fine handmade carpets, others are technicians in oil and chemical refineries. In some parts excellent cotton can be grown, but in most of Turkmenia nothing grows.

Eighty percent of the land is a notorious moonscape desert called the Kara-Kum. A brutal sun fries the desert by day, but at

An early morning street sweeper in Tashkent, Uzbekistan (left) and the Silk Road in Samarkand

night camp fires ward off the chill brought on by rapidly falling temperatures. Sheepherders and horse breeders work next to thriving orchards. A 900-mile (1,450-kilometer) canal is bringing water deep into the desert.

In the snowcapped Tien-Shan mountains of Uzbekistan one can get a suntan in cool air. Miles below in the large, hot, dry capital city of Tashkent a tourist (of which there are many) may have to stop at one of the numerous and beautifully designed water fountains in order to cool off. At Samarkand, another tourist attraction in the Uzbek SSR, one may seek the inside of a turquoise-domed building to retreat from the heat. Both of these ancient, artistic, and fabled desert cities were once stops along the busy Silk Road from China to Europe, but invaders burned them down time and time again. More recently, in 1966, Tashkent was destroyed by an earthquake. But it was again rebuilt and now is a modern city with an up-to-date subway system.

A road leading to Dushanbe, the capital of Tadzhikstan (left)
A collective farmers' market in Tashkent, the capital of Uzbekistan (right)

The main crop in Uzbekistan is cotton. So much is grown there it is called the republic's "white gold." Magnificent silks and the famous astrakhan (Persian lamb) furs are produced in the republic. Rice, grapes, and other fruit are important irrigated farm products. Uzbekistan produces a wide assortment of minerals and manufactures many kinds of machines and equipment. Its most unusual product is a green tea that everyone drinks.

Tadzhikstan is a mountainous country. In the Pamir range, Communism Peak at 24,590 feet (7,495 meters) and Lenin Peak at 23,405 feet (7,113 meters) are the highest mountains in the USSR and rank among the highest in the world. The mountains are also being explored for coal, oil, gas, and other valuable minerals.

In Tadzhikstan, when the snow on the mountain peaks melts each spring, the rapid runoff that used to swell the rivers and flood the fields is controlled by a high dam. The turbulent rivers are put to good use. Electricity is produced and the water is distributed to mountain valleys, making fertile the once-barren land. Cotton, grapes, and fruit are grown there today.

*Moscow, which stretches along both banks of the Moskva River,
is the heart of the USSR and the showcase of the nation. The Kremlin,
shown above, is the seat of government.*

Chapter 7

SPECIAL PLACES

MOSCOW

Moscow is located far from the geographic center of the USSR, but it is at the center of much that takes place in the country. It has been called the heart of Russia, the nation's showcase, Hero City, and the Hub City. The names are appropriate because Moscow is more than the capital of the Union of Soviet Socialist Republics and the Russian Soviet Federated Socialist Republic (RSFSR). This eight-hundred-year-old yet modern city on the banks of the Moskva River is also the political, industrial, cultural, and transportation core of the country. In the Soviet Union all eyes focus on Moscow. All ears listen to its words. And sooner or later everyone wants to visit there.

Life in the capital is similar to life in most other large Soviet cities, except that there is much more to do there. The lines waiting outside shops to purchase hard-to-find items, sometimes including food (especially meats), are similar. There are more automobiles on the streets, but traffic is still quite light. The Moscow buses, streetcars, and taxis all seem crowded. Clusters of people line up at stations to ride them.

People wait in line to enter Lenin's Mausoleum in Red Square.

All Soviet citizens feel a sense of accomplishment about Moscow. It developed like a huge spiderweb fanning out from the center. The Kremlin, St. Basil's Church, and Lenin's Mausoleum in Red Square and the GUM department store are all in the center.

Most visitors head for the metro, which can take them underground to just about every part of the city, including the outlying districts. The Soviet people consider it one of the world's best subway systems.

Buildings in Moscow extend high above the ground. Besides the many new blocks of high-rise apartments and large hotels there is the tall and massive Moscow University. The TV tower in Ostankino projects like a giant needle one third of a mile (one-half kilometer) into the air.

Everyone visiting Moscow wants to tour the Kremlin, where many of the government buildings are located. Once a fortress, it

St. Basil's Church (left) in Red Square was built in the 1500s and Moscow University (right) was built in the 1900s.

is now the country's most important monument to its past and present. Behind the once mysterious Kremlin's walls one can walk back into the excitement of Russian history. There are museums to explore and churches, cathedrals, bell towers, and monasteries to marvel at. The old buildings on the Kremlin grounds are architectural models for studying the past. Their special icons and wall paintings picture times gone by. But the Kremlin has modern buildings, too. The Kremlin Palace of Congresses is a marble and glass structure erected in 1961. It is the seat of the Party Congresses and special national assemblies. It is also used for musical entertainment and seats six thousand people.

Just outside the Kremlin wall on Red Square stands the red and black V.I. Lenin Mausoleum. People from all over the world are willing to stand in a seemingly endless line at any time and in any temperature to inch their way into this hallowed shrine. Once

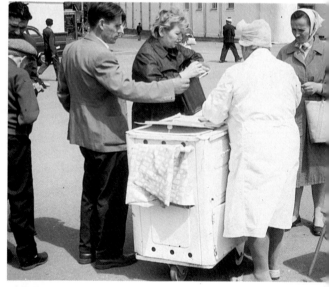

For entertainment in Moscow,
one can go to the
popular Gorki Park Amusement
Center (top), take a trip
on the subway, called the
metro (middle left), buy some
delicious sausages from the
many vendors (middle right),
and browse through the books
for sale at sidewalk
tables (bottom).

Some sights of Moscow include citizens going about their daily activities (top), a trained elephant at the Moscow Circus (middle left), Red Square on a cold winter morning (middle right), and the Kalinin Bridge over the Moskva River.

The GUM department store is located in Red Square. The interior (left) has hundreds of shops and the exterior (shown at the right, above) is very elegant. The building to the left is the State Historical Museum.

inside the tomb they can view the embalmed remains of Lenin.

At the northeast end of Red Square is busy GUM, Moscow's largest department store. Like almost everything else, it is government run. GUM is a two-story building with a glass roof. It resembles an enclosed bazaar with hundreds of undersized shops that open onto long balconies and a shopping mall below. GUM is old-fashioned, but so are most of the stores in the Soviet Union. You must first stand in line to pay for the item you intend to purchase. Then you return to the department with your receipt and wait again. If the item is still in stock, you report to another location to pick it up. More often than not the clerk uses an abacus to make her calculations. Shopping demands a lot of time and patience in the Soviet Union.

There are many museums, art galleries, exhibition halls, and theaters to visit. These fine cultural centers are usually housed in

Leningrad's islands are connected by bridges.

magnificent buildings of splendid architecture. But most elegant of all is the Bolshoi Theater. Its gold interior has magnificent chandeliers, a red curtain, and red seats. For those who enjoy ballet or opera, as many Russians do, being part of the audience at a Bolshoi performance is an experience to be remembered for a lifetime. But other theatergoers may prefer the Moscow State Circus.

LENINGRAD

Leningrad is the second city in the USSR in terms of size and importance. But most Russians think that of it as number one when judged by beauty. Located on the delta of the Neva River, it is built on 101 islands surrounded by smooth rivers and canals. A network of graceful bridges connects the islands, giving the city a touch of Venice. When Peter the Great founded the city in 1703,

The Hermitage (left) is now an art palace, but the original interior (right) is worth seeing in itself.

he received help in its design from outstanding Italian and French architects. Perhaps that is why Leningrad looks more European than Russian.

Today Leningrad is the biggest seaport on the Soviet Baltic Sea, but because of its northern location, the port waters are frozen four months of the year. Therefore, imports from the West, such as grain and other agricultural products, steel pipe, and technical equipment for gas and oil fields, must be shipped in during the warmer months when the port is free of ice.

During the early summer, long hours of daylight give Leningrad a "white night" effect when dusk and dawn appear to blend together. It is especially noticeable around June 21, when the earth is tilted on its axis so that the Northern Hemisphere leans toward the sun. Of course when the opposite holds true during late December, prolonged darkness lingers over Leningrad.

Leningrad is a sort of living legend, a museum city with many places that recapture much of Russia's dramatic history. The

Hydrofoil boats ferry between Leningrad and Petrodvorets.

cruiser *Aurora*, the naval vessel that signaled the beginning of the 1917 revolution, is moored on the Neva River. Peter and Paul Fortress, formerly a tsarist prison, tells much about the power of former Russian rulers. And the famous Admiralty Building, with its golden sailor atop, tells much about how Leningrad has long been influenced by the sea.

At Palace Square stands the majestic pale green and white Winter Palace, now called the Hermitage. It has been converted into one of the world's greatest fine arts museums. A collection of three million items is displayed in four hundred rooms. Masterpieces by world-renowned artists adorn its walls. The interior of the former palace is an art show in its own right.

A fast hydrofoil boat ride away from Leningrad's port is Petrodvorets, the summer palace of Peter the Great on the Gulf of Finland. Its magnificent buildings, gorgeous gardens, and trick

The gardens of Petrodvorets, the summer palace of Peter the Great

fountains show how little the tsars spared in making their surroundings glorious.

However, there is another site that is much more glorious in the minds of Soviet citizens than any Leningrad palace, church, or building. It is the cemetery memorial to the 500,000 who died during the 900-day siege of the city during World War II. The people of Leningrad will never forget their courage and supreme sacrifice.

KIEV

Kiev is the third largest Soviet city. Because it was the ninth century capital of the first state of the Eastern Slavs, it has been called "the mother of Russian cities." Now it is the capital of the Ukrainian republic and a major transportation, industrial, and cultural center.

Kreshchatik, Kiev's main boulevard (left), and a view of Kiev and the Dnieper River from Vladimir Hill

Located on the high green banks of the Dnieper, Europe's third largest river, Kiev is considered to be one of the country's most beautiful cities. It has a kind of picture postcard appearance. Upper town, lower town, and downtown areas are connected by a subway and funicular, a kind of cable railway system. Tall poplar and thick chestnut trees grow on the steep hills, in flower-laden parks, and along the broad avenues and cozy little streets of the city. Many of Kiev's buildings were restored after suffering heavy damage during World War II. They include churches, a famous eleventh century cathedral, a monastery, and the remains of the ancient city's walls and Golden Gate—all masterpieces of a very old culture. Kiev was for centuries the seat of Christianity in Russia.

Unloading logs at Volgograd, a key industrial center (left)
The entrance to the fifteenth-century bazaar in Bukhara (right)

A VARIETY OF CITIES

In a country as vast as the Soviet Union one can expect to find many different types of cities. From Lvov, an industrial city of the Ukraine not far from the Polish border, to Vladivostok, the great naval base and seaport on the Pacific Ocean, hundreds of cities dot the Soviet landscape. These cities, not unlike the people who live in them, vary in size, appearance, and personality.

Many Soviet cities are situated on the banks of rivers. They received their early starts as trading settlements handling goods moving along the rivers. Volgograd, with its key location on the Volga River, is a good example of this. Founded in 1589, it originally was named Tsaritsyn. Today it is a city specializing in tractor building and chemical and food industries.

Ashkhabad and Bukhara, desert oases in central Asia, also developed as transport junctions. They were crossroad stops for merchant caravans of camels bearing goods bound for Russia, India, and China. Now they are important agricultural and industrial centers.

More than three hundred rivers and streams flow into Lake Baikal.

VILLAGES

Russian villages tend to be clusters of houses, barns, and sheds closely connected to each other by wood fences and backyard paths. They often straddle a dirt or gravel road that leads to another village during the kinder months of the year. Deep winter snows and the soft gluelike mud of spring can turn a village into a temporary prison for six months of the year.

SPECIAL PLACES

There are three special places of which the people of the Soviet Union are particularly proud. They are all located in Siberia. One is a very old natural site, Lake Baikal. Another is a man-made marvel called Akademgorodok. The third, a railroad, is a dynamic example of how people are changing nature to such an extent that the future of all of the USSR will be affected.

LAKE BAIKAL

Lake Baikal is almost one mile (1.6 kilometers) deep and extends for 400 miles (640 kilometers) in length and up to 49 miles (79 kilometers) in width. Its basin contains 20 percent of all the freshwater resources on the planet. Lake Baikal contains 80 percent of the USSR's freshwater supply. Some 336 rivers and streams empty into the lake.

AKADEMGORODOK

Akademgorodok, which means "Academic Town," is located 15 miles (25 kilometers) south of Novosibirsk, Siberia's largest city. It is a special national research center—a kind of "think-tank" town. Its setting is the shore of a large artificial lake, the Ob Reservoir, nestled in a forest of pine and birch trees. As many as 54,000 people live and work there in an atmosphere that resembles a well-planned college campus. Life is quite comfortable for Akademgorodok's 15,000 scientists and technicians and their families.

Most live in large well-constructed attractive apartments or cottages, amid five shopping centers, clubs, theaters, libraries, sports facilities, and medical centers. Residents can easily walk or ride their bikes along the tree-lined avenues to any one of the twenty-three large research institutes or laboratories. The beauty, high living standards, and attention given Akademgorodok help explain why it is often called "Russia's favorite child."

Some of the country's brightest and most highly respected scientists are sent to Akademgorodok to conduct research and try to solve all kinds of physical and human problems facing Siberia, the USSR, and the rest of the world. The most gifted and talented

A crew of workers repairing the Trans-Siberian Railroad tracks.

high school scientists and mathematicians are invited to take up residence there, too. As young scholars they are instructed by the nation's top scientists while being put through the most challenging curriculum in all of the Soviet Union.

THE BAIKAL-AMUR MAINLINE

The Baikal-Amur Mainline (BAM) was completed in October, 1984. It is of tremendous importance to Siberia and all of the USSR. It connects Lake Baikal with the Amur River in the Soviet Far East, a distance of 2,000 miles (3,200 kilometers). The new railroad runs from 100 to 200 miles (160 to 320 kilometers) north of the overburdened Trans-Siberian Railroad. Started in 1974, it was an incredible task. Most of the route is in the permafrost zone. Parts of mountains had to be blown away. Ice valleys had to be crossed. Tunnels, some up to 9 miles (14 kilometers) long, had to be dug. Miles of bridges had to be constructed. Snow and ice blocks 1,000 feet (305 meters) deep had to be melted by jet flames. There were other hardships and battles for the tens of thousands of workers. Aside from the cold winter and the devastating attacks by swarms of mosquitoes in the summer, the work brigades had to contend with over 1,500 earthquakes.

BAM carries vital fuels, minerals, and timber across the Siberian taiga to the industrial centers.

Soviet people follow a variety of religions. Above left: Preparing for a baptismal service in an Armenian Gregorian church. Above right: A Muslim elder of Tashkent reads inside the mosque grounds. Below left: The interior of the Bukhara Jewish Synagogue in Uzbekistan. Below right: Mass being celebrated in the Roman Catholic church of St. Ludovik in Moscow

Chapter 8

EVERYDAY LIFE

THE PEOPLE

More than one hundred nationalities live in the Soviet Union, the third largest country in the world in population (after China and India). Russians make up only about half of the total number of people living in the USSR. One person in five is Ukrainian. All Soviet nationalities have their own carefully preserved history, art, language, and tradition. The language used throughout most of the Soviet Union is Russian, but each republic has its own official language. In all, 130 different languages are spoken.

Atheism, the belief that there is no God, is officially encouraged, but millions of people still believe in the Russian Orthodox church teachings. Other religious groups in the country include Muslims, Buddhists, Evangelical Christian Baptists, Lutherans, Roman Catholics, Jews, Old Believers, and members of the Armenian church.

Soviet citizens work an average of forty hours a week and receive a vacation of from two weeks to a month each year. Both parents in a family usually work; it is not uncommon for them to take separate vacations. More women than men hold jobs and they do almost any kind of work except mining. Seventy-five percent of the doctors are women. Many women are engineers and scientists. Women are usually responsible for shopping, which often includes time standing in line waiting to be served.

FOOD

What you eat in the Soviet Union depends upon your nationality, what is available in the market, and where you live. In the southern republics the food is often similar to dishes from Turkey and Greece. Lamb pieces, kebobs (*shashlyk*), and sausages on skewers cooked over an open fire are a delight for many, especially in Georgia. So too are a variety of chicken and fish dishes cooked on the spit and topped with melted cheese or nuts. In Siberia, where canned fish, horse, and reindeer meat is eaten, there may also be some Oriental-style flavorings and side dishes to satisfy native tastes. In central Asia, *plov*, a mutton and rice mixture, is popular.

The teapot or family samovar, the ever present Russian urn for making tea, supplies the beverage for the meal. Tea in Russia is called *chi*, which obviously refers to its place of origin, China. Vodka is in great demand. Wine is also found in most homes.

NATIONALITIES AND MINORITIES OF THE SOVIET UNION

With the movement of workers from villages to cities and from farms to factories, great changes are taking place in the cultural heritage of the Soviet peoples. Radio and television broadcasts beamed via satellites all over the country tend to make certain aspects of living in the USSR rather alike. Though a modern Soviet culture is developing rapidly, many nationalities and minorities continue to cling to some of their past ways.

Carpets woven in Ashkhabad are world renowned.

Many minorities still excel in time-proven specialties handed down from father to son over the generations. Jews are often highly educated and make outstanding contributions to the country's professions, arts, and sciences. Mordovians, from the Volga valley, are famous as master beekeepers. The Evenk tribes of the north are superior hunters. Yakuts, from Siberia, are expert at fishing in fast-moving streams. The Chukchi can handle twenty thousand head of reindeer on their Arctic farms. Both the Yakuts and Chukchis are skilled ivory carvers. The Tuvinians have been noted for their talents in cross-country skiing and fur trapping in Siberia.

The Tatars are known for their architecture. Latvians are great sailors. Lithuanians know how to grow delicious fruit and Estonians have a folk music tradition. The Armenians are respected as artisans, scientists, and clever merchants. The Ukrainians are hard working on their productive collective farms and in their factory enterprises. The people of Turkmenia and the other central Asian republics turn out unique high-quality carpets, while the Kazakhs have for centuries been admired as skilled horsemen.

The different nationalities and minorities in the Soviet Union tend to retain many of their special skills, traits, and customs.

*Building a mud hut in Samarkand (left), and peasant homes
with a collective farm field in the background*

HOMES

During World War II more than six million homes were
destroyed throughout Russia. That was almost half of the housing.
In rebuilding the country new industries were started all over the
land. New cities sprang up rapidly. Apartments were needed
immediately for the workers. Millions of flats were constructed,
but there is still a serious housing shortage in the Soviet Union.
Yet the fast pace of apartment building continues.

Most of the single-family homes that remain in the cities are
used to their fullest until new apartments are ready. Sometimes
they house more than one family. Each family may be required to
share a kitchen and bathroom.

In the villages, especially in Russia and Siberia, the homes are
constructed of wood or logs taken from nearby forests. The
windows of village homes are often quite decorative. They are
enclosed by hand-carved frames usually painted blue. In the small
fenced-in backyard gardens of these country homes the villagers
plant vegetables, grapevines, and sunflowers. Nearby a cow might
be grazing next to the family-owned chickens, geese, and ducks.

Young Pioneers in Moscow

YOUTH ORGANIZATIONS

Not everyone in the USSR is asked to join the Communist party. However, the chance of being a member of the party is greater if a person proves to have an outstanding record as a member of the Komsomol, the mass organization of young people between the ages of fourteen and twenty-eight. This Young Communist League has a membership of 36 million.

Another young organization, the Young Pioneers, unites 25 million children between ten and fifteen years of age. The Young Pioneers is composed of units and brigades, each attached to a local Komsomol cell. Principles of communism are taught. The children become involved in helping their communities. They also go on field trips, write wall newspapers, attend special clubs, pursue hobbies, and participate in talent festivals and sport and military games.

In some ways the Young Pioneers activities are not unlike those found in American 4-H clubs or scouting groups. But the Pioneers have become arms of the state and are deeply involved in assisting schools in ideological and patriotic indoctrination of children. The organization has its own red banner, unit flags, badges, salute, and a distinguishing red necktie, a three-cornered red scarf that

An English class in Leningrad (left) and students from Tbilisi State University in Georgia (right)

symbolizes the unity of the Pioneers with the Komsomol and Communist party. The children are taught honesty, modesty, courage, and responsibility for citizenship in the USSR. Discipline, respect, and work skills are emphasized.

Being a member of Komsomol is a kind of training ground for being a practicing Communist. It also opens doors to job promotions, university admissions, and careers as military officers that may be closed to young people who were never in Komsomol.

EDUCATION

Education in the USSR is compulsory. Formal education begins for everyone at age six and usually continues until age seventeen. Most Soviet children attend preschools beginning at three years of age, especially if they have working parents and no *babushka* (grandmother) to look after them. More than likely they attend a nursery run by a factory, collective farm, enterprise, or trade union.

The courses of study throughout the USSR are generally quite similar, except that the various republics include studies about their national or regional customs and heritage. Non-Russian peoples have the right for their children to be taught in their native tongues. Though textbooks may be written in as many as fifty-two different languages, the same basic material is covered in a rather standard curriculum. That program is developed and controlled by the government's Ministry of Education in Moscow. The required courses of study run through the tenth grade. Soviet children are not pampered in school. Much is expected of them. Schoolwork is difficult and is to be taken seriously.

SPECIALIZED SCHOOLS

The Soviet system recognizes the need for many kinds of specialized schools. Children having outstanding skills, abilities, or talents are identified early. They are encouraged to attend a special purpose school. These schools might stress military cadet training, ballet, sports and gymnastics, music, certain technical and vocational courses, or even circus and theater arts. But no matter what type of school Soviet students attend, they must take a national examination at the end of the eighth grade. The scores they receive could, more than anything else, determine the level and kind of high school they will be able to enter. The best schools, which prepare students for university and, eventually professional studies, require the highest grades. Lower scoring students go on to technical or vocational high schools and find work in factories, stores, or on state farms. There are about 6,500 vocational schools in the USSR. Many provide instruction in a trade and complete secondary education.

May Day celebration in Red Square, Moscow

Chapter 9

CUSTOMS, HOLIDAYS, SPORTS, AND RECREATION

Before the USSR became such a huge multinational state, the most popular holidays in Russia were religious. Now, under the Communist government, many of these observances have changed, but some customs remain. Certain people, especially those who are older or live in villages and towns, still cling to some of their past practices, be they Christian or Muslim. Jews are considered to be a nationality in the Soviet Union, but interest in their religion and traditions persists.

HOLIDAYS

Easter continues to be widely celebrated in Russia, as it has been for generations. Russians still gather in churchyards at midnight on Easter Eve to light candles and sing religious songs. Women have their Easter cakes blessed by the local priest. People paint beautiful designs on eggs for the Easter feast.

Though Christmas has become less important than the New Year holiday, some customs of the season are still celebrated. In

*Intricately decorated
Ukrainian Easter eggs*

the Ukraine carols are sung, trees are decorated, and hay is placed about the floor to commemorate the fact that Christ was born in a manger. The *kolach*, a three-tier braided Christmas bread with a candle on it, is set on the holiday food table. Twelve meatless dishes are served before the midnight mass. Prior to the meal the children go outside to look for the first star of the evening — the Christmas star.

Christmas is not an official holiday in the Soviet Union. People mark the New Year instead, observing traditions associated in the West with Christmas, including decorating trees and exchanging gifts. The holiday spirit lasts for the first two weeks in January. The children are particularly happy, for this is the holiday when a red-clad Grandfather Frost, a kind of first cousin to Santa Claus, pays a visit. With his assistant, the Snow Maiden, he puts toys and gifts around the tree on New Year's Day.

The two most important legal holidays in the USSR are November 7 and May 1; both are two-day holidays. November 7 is the anniversary of the successful Bolshevik uprising. May 1 (May Day) is a day to honor all workers. On both days great rallies and parades are held in cities throughout the country. The one in Red Square on November 7 outside the Kremlin gates has become a mass demonstration of Soviet military might.

A gymnast performs on the parallel bars as his coach watches.

CUSTOMS

The people in the Soviet Union have two special customs that show enthusiastic ways of expressing their feelings. Greeting a friend or saying good-bye is usually accompanied by a bear hug and the traditional three kisses on the cheek. It is also the custom to show appreciation for a performance by clapping loudly in a rhythmic beat. The person being applauded also joins in the clapping to show his or her thanks to the audience.

SPORTS AND RECREATION

The development of the body by education, discipline, and training is so important in the USSR that it is actually encouraged by the constitution. Mass "physical culture" is required at every level of school instruction, from kindergarten through university. More than 220,000 sports clubs and societies are organized all over the country.

Young people in the Soviet Union are very active in competitive sports. Boys and girls between nine and fourteen with outstanding

Archery is a popular sport in Georgia.

athletic abilities can enroll in one of 5,500 specialized junior sports schools. With few exceptions, most Soviet sports stars come from such schools. Once every two years a nationwide olympiad is held for schoolchildren. Every four years the USSR Games are staged, with athletic competition in twenty-five different sports. The winners often go on to compete in international events, including the Olympics.

Today Soviets can participate in sixty-six different sporting activities. Soccer, basketball, and track and field are the most popular. Volleyball games are also actively engaged in at camps, picnics, and beaches. Popular individual sports include cross-country skiing, skating, fishing, and hunting. The Soviets love to play chess. Gymnastics, wrestling, and ice hockey have received much attention of late. Mechanized sports, such as motor car and

Young chess players (left), and students of the Moscow Academic Ballet School (right) performing Coppelia *by Delibes*

motorcycle racing, gliding, scuba diving, and motor boat racing, are catching on, too.

Many different forms of recreation are offered in the USSR besides sporting events. Animals draw crowds at aquariums and zoos and just about every major city has a circus. There are many theaters in the Soviet Union with a wide choice of productions to meet almost any taste, ranging from tragedies to comedies. Moscow has a Theater for Young Spectators; elsewhere throughout the land more than a hundred puppet theaters bring smiles and laughs to young audiences.

The Soviet opera and ballet theaters have a long history of excellence. The Bolshoi Ballet is more than two hundred years old. The company of one thousand has toured throughout the world. To become a leading dancer in the Bolshoi or Kirov troup is the ultimate dream of countless girls and boys.

НЕГРАМОТНЫЙ тот-же СЛЕПОЙ

A poster used to fight against illiteracy reads, "An illiterate
is also blind. Everywhere failure and unhappiness await him."
The Russian language uses the Cyrillic alphabet, which is
mainly based on the Greek alphabet.

Chapter 10

LITERATURE, MUSIC, AND THE PERFORMING ARTS

LITERATURE

The Russian people are heirs to a great literary tradition and reputation. Respect for writers and poets continues to this day in the Soviet Union. Poems, novels, and other published works often cause readers to think, discuss, and act. This power of the pen is one of the reasons why Communist officials concern themselves with what is being written. The government tries to pressure writers not to publish anything that disagrees with government policy. It has been that way since the Revolution of 1917. Soviet writers belong to the Union of Writers of the USSR, which was established in 1932.

During the early Soviet period Konstantin A. Fedin, Leonid M. Loenov, and Alexander Fadeyev aroused a great amount of interest with their novels. Later, a famous book entitled *And Quiet Flows the Don* by Mikhail A. Sholokhov was published. Its hero is a brave cossack who tries to sort out his life and his fate under the enormous pressures of war and revolution. To this day there is controversy as to whether or not Sholokhov really wrote this great book or took the manuscript from someone else.

During the 1920s and 1930s, a large number of prose writers were active in Soviet Russian literature. Mikhail Bulgakov wrote a series of very sharp satires, followed by *The Master and Margarita*, one of the greatest novels written in this century. The humorous defiance in the novel was so strong that it was not published until the 1960s, over twenty years after Bulgakov's death.

Mikhail Zoshchenko published short, biting stories that poked fun at everyday pretensions and pompous propaganda. His work was for a long time the most popular reading among average Soviet citizens. They loved his popular story-telling style.

Isaak Babel was a Jewish writer who evoked the colorful Jewish section of his native port city, Odessa, with all of its good-natured fun and mischief. He also described the early days of the Soviet army and its cossack riders in *Red Cavalry and Other Stories*.

One of Russia's most distinguished writers and poets of the twentieth century was Boris Pasternak. Copies of his 1957 novel, *Doctor Zhivago*, were hard to find in the Soviet state, but the book was widely circulated and read abroad. The book was made into a very popular motion picture. In 1958 Pasternak won the Nobel Prize in literature, but refused to accept it, fearing he might have to leave his beloved Russia forever.

In 1962 Alexander Solzhenitsyn published *One Day in the Life of Ivan Denisovich* in the Soviet Union. It describes the experiences of inmates in a Stalin era prison camp. At that time the Soviet leaders were reacting against Stalin's abuse of power. Solzhenitsyn wrote other novels about people with extraordinary strength and heroism. When he, too, received the Nobel Prize (in 1970), he was prohibited from accepting it until after the Soviet

Mikhail A. Sholokhov (left) and Alexander Solzhenitsyn (right)

government exiled him in 1974 and he moved to Switzerland. Later he decided to live in the United States, retreating to a farm in Vermont.

Poetry recitals, in which poets read their poems before large audiences, are very popular in the Soviet Union. Poetry Day is celebrated in December each year with many public readings by poets.

Vladimir Mayakovsky was the most colorful and unusual poet to support the revolution. He showered defiance and humorous barbs like verbal fireworks upon friends and foes alike, using colorful and very unusual language.

Vladimir Mayakovsky

Osip Mandelshtam was a great practitioner of the classical, rich, ringing Russian language. His poetry has the power of great music. He was killed in a prison camp in 1938. In spite of the fact that his poetry was not republished until the mid-1970s, it has been the rallying point of educated Russians for over two generations since his death.

Anna Akhmatova was the poetic voice of Russian feeling and sensibility. She dared to write about the feelings of relatives of those who were arrested by Stalin's government, especially in Leningrad. Her extraordinary poem "Requiem" is dedicated to that great city and its troubles. Until her death in 1966, Ahkmatova was a proud and widely admired figure among Soviet intellectuals and writers.

There are many other poets. Sergei Esenin celebrated old-fashioned Russia in a modernistic, brawling style. Maria Tsvetaeva wrote in a beautiful and popular lyric vein.

In the years that followed the revolution, a few courageous, creative poets departed from the strict Communist themes. One of the best-known poets, Yevgeni Yevtushenko, wrote about becoming corrupt with the easy life and the mistreatment of certain people. Andrei Voznesensky composed soul-searching verse about the harshness of city life. Nikolai Tikhonov showed his independence in realistic poems about romantic subjects. Many poets and novelists wrote about war themes and episodes. Others dealt with philosophy and ethics.

Soviet playwrights have contributed many kinds of plays for staging throughout the country. In the 1920s and 1930s dramas with Communist messages predominated. Plays about the war followed. More recently a wider range of plays has appeared. Some deal with satire and comedy, while others center on life's problems and love themes. Outstanding plays have been written by Nikolai Pogodin, Vera Panova, Leonid Zorin, Viktor Rozov, Alexander Volodin, Aleksei Arbuzov, and Yevgeni Shvarts.

FILMMAKING

The film classic *Battleship Potemkin* made by Sergei Eisenstein in 1925 is considered by many to be one of the best films ever made. Now, filmmaking has become very important in the Soviet Union. More than three hundred full-length films are produced each year. Every day eleven to twelve million people all over the country go to see films.

A billboard advertising the movie "The Heart of Russia"

MUSIC

Soviet musical composers and artists have followed a great tradition of Russian excellence in musical science and performance. The love of fine music is great in the USSR. There are 150 philharmonic societies and over 700 symphony orchestras in the Soviet Union. Every year their concerts are attended by millions of people. Chamber music is also very popular.

Two very gifted composers, Dmitri Shostakovich and Sergei Prokofiev, have had tremendous influence on musical composition in the world today. Aram Khachaturian, an Armenian composer born in Georgia, is popular in the Soviet Union and abroad. His "Saber Dance" is familiar to music lovers everywhere. Other important Soviet composers are Dmitri Kabalevsky, Ivan Dzeryhinsky, and Tikhon Khrenikov. A number of Russian composers, including Rachmaninoff, Stravinsky, and

A Ukrainian trio entertains on banduras, popular folk musical instruments.

Grechaninov, left their country after the revolution and settled in the United States. Conductors and performers; among them Serge Koussevitsky, Vladimir Horowitz, Jascha Heifetz, Mstislav Rostropovich, and Nathan Milstein, left as well.

RECOGNITION OF ARTISTS

Many great Soviet artists are invited to perform throughout the world. They include some of the most talented musical soloists, orchestras, ballet companies, and dance troupes. Their performances are acclaimed.

Each year in the Soviet Union outstanding literary works and contributions in the fields of music and the performing arts are nominated for Lenin Prizes and state prizes. These high awards bring great honor and recognition. They are cherished for life.

Workers prepare the
pipeline that transports
natural gas from
Siberia to Europe (above).
A generator assembly
in Leningrad (left)

Chapter 11

THE ECONOMY

The Soviet Union is a great industrial power, second only to the United States. However, the economic systems of the two nations are quite different. The United States and most other Western countries operate under a system in which the land, factories, and various means for producing goods are owned and operated by individuals for profit. This is known as capitalism.

In the USSR the government owns all the land, the natural resources, and the means of production. Individuals are not allowed to own land, banks, retail stores, or factories. Business transactions normally are centrally controlled according to a national plan. Profit making is not generally permitted. It is against the law to hire workers to labor for another individual's benefit. Under the Soviet system as originally designed, all the people were expected to share in the work and the goods produced. This kind of system is called communism.

LONG-TERM PLANS

The economy of the USSR is set by long-term plans, usually covering periods of five years. The first five-year plan started in 1929; since then industrial growth has been increasing at a high

Preparing leather at a leather goods factory in Armenia

rate. Today the USSR leads the world in the production of cement, pig iron, petroleum, coal, steel, iron, manganese, and locomotives. It also out-produces all other countries in the production of cotton, flax, fertilizers, woolen fabrics, leather footwear, sugar, and butter.

Sometimes the goals of the national plans are not met. Many unexpected problems can slow things up and prevent the reaching of production quotas. This can result in shortages of consumer goods, the items people buy for their daily needs. Sometimes Soviet people spend long hours shopping for products that are not always available in every store. On the other hand, today when they find what they are after, they are more confident that the product will be made better and will be available in a variety of styles and sizes. In the past Soviet buyers often complained about the quality and kinds of goods being manufactured.

AGRICULTURE

Soviet agriculture lags far behind industry. It is the weakest part of the nation's economy, despite the fact that the Soviet Union

The orchard and homes on a collective farm

ranks first in the world in a number of food crops. How to provide the large population with more than a basic amount of food remains the country's most serious problem, as it has for centuries past. The main farming regions are often hit by droughts. When the grain harvest is poor, livestock can't be fed unless grain is purchased from other countries. Because of shortages, the Soviet diet is usually very low on meat and dairy products. When available, meat is very expensive. In the wintertime fresh vegetables and fruit are not very plentiful. People rely on bread, starches, sausages, canned fish, cabbage, and beets in preparing their meals.

There are three different economies in Soviet agriculture: the state farm (*sovkhoz*), the collective farm (*kolkhoz*), and the small private garden plot the member of a collective or state farm is allowed to own. State farms operate about two thirds of the farmland of the USSR. They are owned and operated by the state, or government, and their workers are paid employees. They tend to be very large and are run like big outdoor factories. Each averages about 50,000 acres (20,200 hectares) in size (130 times

A private vegetable plot outside the wall of a monastery in Suzdal, north of Moscow

larger than the average United States farm) and needs about six hundred workers. Many specialize in meat and milk production.

Collective farms are usually smaller than state farms and engage in many types of agriculture. On a collective farm the government owns the land but leases it to a unit of farmers, averaging 460 households per farm. The farm is worked under the direction of a committee headed by a chairman who is really in charge of the farm's operation. All equipment, buildings, and livestock are owned by the collective, which is often made up of several villages. Like the state farms the collectives sell most of their produce to the government at a set price. At the end of each month a worker is paid according to the amount of work done for the farm. His share comes from the sale of the farm's output after expenses are paid.

The private plots are becoming more important in the USSR.

*A collective farmers' market in Tashkent (left),
and a Georgian shepherd with his flock*

The farmers spend a lot of time cultivating their own gardens.
Though less then 2 percent of all agricultural land is worked
privately, it is estimated that 30 percent of the production of
vegetables, potatoes, meat, milk, and eggs comes from this source.
Many farmers raise poultry on their private lots. Most of the
produce is kept by the plot owners themselves. The rest is sold on
the free market for higher prices to buyers interested in better
quality food. The farmers keep the profits.

Though the territory of the Soviet Union is vast, less than a
quarter of it can be used for agricultural production. Most of the
food is grown in European Russia. Wheat comes mostly from the
Ukraine, Kazakhstan, and southwestern Siberia. Cotton is a
product of central Asia. Tea, the national beverage, grows along
the Black Sea coast and sunflowers do well in the Donets and Ural
regions.

Hydroelectric power station in the Caucasus Mountains

INDUSTRY

The Soviet industrial system also involves state control and centralized planning. Just about every kind of manufactured product has been made in the country. Thousands of plants turn out both heavy and light industry products—from farm combines to cigarettes and copper wire to cotton threads. The main concentration of industry is also in European Russia, but lately Soviet planners are trying to introduce industrialization to other parts of the Soviet Union, especially where local resources are found. Manufacturing is growing by leaps and bounds. Automation of factories is taking place. Many large thermal, atomic, and hydroelectric power stations supply great amounts of electricity all over the land. In recent years there has been rapid growth in the instrument building, aerospace, laser, super pure metals and other scientific and technical industries. Computers are being manufactured for use on thousands of projects throughout the country.

More and more industrial goods are being exported. The USSR is a major supplier of metal-manufacturing, power-generating, and chemical equipment. Exports also include complete factories,

Sturgeon fishing season on the Volga River. Some of the famous Russian caviar is made from the salted eggs of the sturgeon.

machine tools, tractors, motor vehicles, ships, and aircraft. The Soviet Union has also been selling diamonds, jewelry, and military weapons abroad.

NATURAL RESOURCES

The Soviet Union's amazing growth into one of the world's leading industrial powers is credited to its good fortune of having a wealth of natural resources. Practically every major mineral can be found within its boundaries. There are coal mines and gold mines, fields with bauxite and fields with chromite, magnesium pits and manganese pits, and even silver and sulfur. The Soviet Union is rich in fuel supplies, especially natural gas, as well as petroleum. Soviet gas is exported to Europe.

Three additional natural resources have proved important for the economy of the USSR: the forest, furs, and fish. The Soviet Union leads all other nations in lumbering. Perhaps as much as 20 percent of the world's timber is located in the Soviet Union, and over 80 percent of that is found in Siberia. So vast are these reserves that the taiga region is referred to as the "green ocean."

Fur coats are great for keeping warm during the winter.

The fur industry has always been highly developed in Russia. Fur trapping and hunting extend over nearly one half of the Soviet Union, but are mostly done in Siberia. Almost all is carried out during the winter months. Fur farms are becoming valuable sources for many kinds of pelts, some of which are exported after being processed and sold in Leningrad. Mink, ermine, and fox are highly valued and rare, but astrakhan (Persian lamb), squirrel, and muskrat are sold in much greater quantities.

Soviet fishermen are active all over the world. Vessels flying the red flag of the USSR spend months on end exploring the waters of the Indian, Atlantic, and Pacific oceans. Some trawlers have the capacity to serve as giant seagoing "fish factories." Tons of catch are quickly cut up, processed, and canned or frozen aboard ship. The floating bases return to their home ports only after their holds are full. Closer to home, in the cold Barents and White seas, cod, haddock, herring, and salmon are caught. Delicious sturgeon is found in the warmer waters of the Caspian Sea. The famous and expensive caviar is the salted eggs of sturgeon. Russia's thousands of streams, rivers, and lakes are fishable every month of the year.

Whales are still caught for their oil in Pacific Ocean waters off the Kamchatka Peninsula.

ENERGY PRODUCTION

A nation, no matter how wealthy in natural resources, cannot develop its industrial economy without energy and an efficient and reliable transportation system. The first Soviet planners realized that when drawing their blueprint for industrial progress upon seizing power in 1917.

The Soviet Union is the only major industrial country that appears to be self-sufficient in energy production. Before the Russian Revolution remote places relied on wood as an energy source to fire steam engines. Oil lamps were used for lighting. Now, such natural resources as coal, oil, natural gas, and water, all in plentiful supply, are used for generating electric power. Nuclear power stations have been constructed. On the Arctic Ocean, near Murmansk, the force of the tides is used to generate power. And in the warmer and sunnier parts of the USSR there are experiments in solar energy use.

The Soviet Union is noted for its great potential for hydroelectric power, about 80 percent of it being in Asia, Siberia, and the Far East. The world's largest hydroelectric station is located near Krasnoyarsk on the Yenisey River in Siberia. For the long-term planners there is an interesting problem that must be solved in the years ahead. Should new industrial plants be built in Siberia where there are many kinds of energy reserves? Or should the industries remain primarily in European Russia, with the energy and natural resources transported to that region of the country? In either event people or power will have to be moved.

In large cities, buses are a common means of transportation, but in the country older forms of transportation, such as this donkey cart in Samarkand (left), are still in use.

TRANSPORATION

Past modes of surface transportation—sleds, wagons, and carriages pulled by dogs, mules, horses, and reindeer—have largely given way to motorized vehicles. The bus has become the number one intercity transporter of people in the Soviet Union. Buses carry more than three times as many passengers as do the railways and one hundred times as many as the airlines.

Relatively few people own private cars and most of those who do use them only four to five months a year during the warm season. With extended periods of ice and snow and few service stations between cities, driving can prove to be quite hazardous. Hard-surface roads are expensive to build and difficult to keep up in the cold climate regions of the USSR. That is why road building is not as important as pipeline building, or railways and aviation, especially in the newly developed areas of Siberia and the Soviet Far East.

A train traveling along Lake Sevan in Armenia (left). Part of the Aeroflot fleet, estimated at over two thousand planes, at Sheremetyevo Airport, Moscow (right)

The USSR has one tenth of the world's railway tracks, but it accounts for more than half of the world's total rail freight traffic. Trucks carry mostly short haul farm products or manufactured cargo, but only about 8 percent of all freight is transported over Soviet roads on trucks. Since the 1960s most of the Soviet Union's oil and gas has been transported by growing networks of pipelines from major deposits in Siberia to the western Soviet Union and eastward to the Pacific coast.

The Soviet merchant marine is also growing rapidly. Traditionally, Russia was a landlocked country with few opportunities to trade with countries overseas. Now Soviet vessels sail the seven seas. In the last few years the USSR has established herself as a leading maritime power despite the fact that she has few ports, most of which are not free of ice in the winter. The long Arctic coast is icebound about nine months of the year, but in 1977 the world's most powerful atomic icebreaker, the *Artika*, broke a path to the North Pole. It took the Soviet ship thirteen days and nights to get to the top of the world and return to Murmansk, its home base. It sailed a total of 3,852 nautical miles (4,436 statute miles), of which 1,200 (1,380 statute miles) were through solid ice. The possibility of opening frozen sea-lanes in the Arctic is very important to the Soviet Union as it races to develop new frontier regions of the Arctic and Siberia.

All major rivers in the USSR flow through flat country, but they too are frozen from four to ten months of the year, depending on their location and latitude. That is why river transport accounts for a relatively small part of the country's freight traffic. In an attempt to move more materials and goods more rapidly and consistently, more boats and barges have been added to the interior "river highway" fleets.

In the summertime people often visit a busy spot along one of the 42,000 miles (67,600 kilometers) of rivers and canals operating in the USSR and watch the boat parade. Hydrofoils streak past steamers at 60 miles (97 kilometers) an hour. Haggard tugs pushing barges whistle at attractive tourist ships. Seagoing ore ships and freighters sail side by side with local passenger ferries. And on the Siberian rivers thousands of timber logs float downstream to the nearest lumber mill.

Aeroflot, the national airline of the USSR, is the largest airline in the world. It flies to eighty countries and carries about 25 percent of all the world's air passengers on some of the newest and most advanced aircraft. Each year more than 100 million passengers fly somewhere in its 621,371-mile (1,000,000-kilometer) flight paths.

Aeroflot carries millions of tons of cargo, too. Throughout the country planes are able to fly over harsh climatic conditions that bring other forms of transportation to a standstill. Airplanes deliver construction materials to new building sites in remote areas. Helicopters lay rail lines and pipelines. Helicopters and fixed-wing aircraft fly machinery to mines and factories.

Typical Russian onion domes on a church in Moscow

Geologists use them for prospecting. They patrol against potential
forest fires, always a major threat in the timberlands. They drop
grain seeds over farm fields and dust and spray chemicals over
crops. They deliver mail, food, and equipment to isolated outposts.
They evacuate sick villagers in emergencies, and drop supplies to
Siberian reindeer herders once serviced only by dogsled.

Transporting people and goods in a country the size of the
USSR has not been an easy task. But to her credit much has been
accomplished in mastering distance and overcoming natural
barriers. In recent times Soviet engineers, scientists, and
transportation specialists have made remarkable progress on land,
sea, and air. Beneath the ground marvelous subways have been
built.

Left: New housing under construction in the Moscow area.
Above: A construction worker
Below: In 1984 some World War II veterans held a reunion.

Chapter 12

COMPLETING THE TWENTIETH CENTURY

DOMESTIC AFFAIRS

In the 1980s Soviet officials initiated new actions to prevent citizens from violating laws or going against government policies. The power of the KGB state security force was increased. A campaign was started to penalize more severely people found guilty of taking bribes or getting involved in corruption for personal gain.

The number of citizens permitted to emigrate declined significantly from previous years. Those who demonstrated that they wished to do so, or applied for an exit visa, continued to face loss of their jobs. A few Soviet citizens, while visiting abroad, chose not to return home to the USSR. Because of this, their citizenship was revoked.

Campaigns publicized the fact that Soviet women were overworked and had too many responsibilities. In addition to their jobs, they were often expected to take care of the children, do the cleaning, cooking, and laundry, and spend many hours waiting in long lines shopping for food and other family necessities.

Attempts were also undertaken by the government to have Soviet citizens cut down or refrain from drinking too much. But alcoholism remained the main social problem in the Soviet Union.

In housing, the Soviet Union has made great strides in overcoming the shortage of apartments, or flats as they are often called. In most cities throughout the country, blocks and blocks of high-rise apartment buildings are being constructed. Now in Moscow, for example, more than five hundred families move into new apartments each day. Many take residence in the hundreds of attractive white tower, micro-district complexes that are starting to ring the capital. These are self-contained, multistory structures that offer every type of need and service to the residents.

In a national outpouring of special appreciation and gratitude, on May 9, 1985 the Soviet Union commemorated the fortieth anniversary of their victory over the Nazi invading armies during the Great Patriotic War (World War II). Millions of Soviet citizens paid tribute to the men and women who served in the armed forces or who helped in many different ways to defeat the enemy. Military parades, rallies, pageants, and memorial programs were held in practically every city, town, and village in the USSR. People visited cemeteries and paid their respects to heroes by placing floral wreaths at the base of monuments and statues throughout the land.

EXPANDED SPACE EXPLORATION

The Soviet Union's record of accomplishments in space exploration remained very impressive. In 1984 new crews of

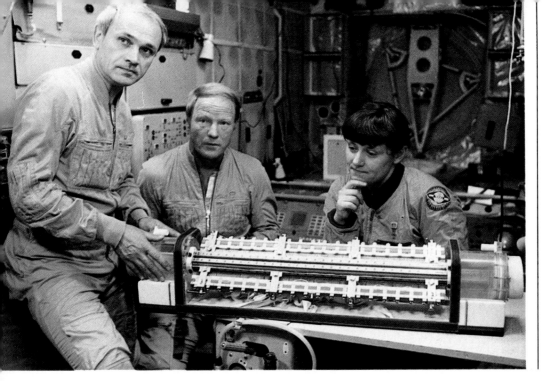

The Soyuz T-12 *crew; V.A. Dzhanibekov, I.P. Volk, and S. Ye. Savitskaya, the first woman to walk in space*

cosmonauts were launched from the Soviet space center at Baikonur in Kazakhstan in Central Asia. In that year three separate manned spacecraft, *Soyuz T-10, T-11,* and *T-12* were sent up to dock with the orbiting space station *Salyut 7.* Their crews conducted scientific experiments in outer space. During the July mission in that series, Svetlana Savitskaya became the first woman to walk in space. On October 2, 1984 three Soviet cosmonauts returned to the earth in *Soyuz T-11* after spending a record 237 days in space.

In June of 1985 planetary weather balloons with instrument packages began sending data on the clouds and winds of Venus after being dropped into the planet's atmosphere by *Vega-1* and *Vega-2.* These Soviet spacecraft were en route to a meeting with Halley's comet in March, 1986.

The exploration balloon, a first of its kind, floated at an altitude of about 33 miles (53 kilometers) above the surface of Venus. It transmitted signals revealing scientific data about atmospheric conditions there. The signals were "read" 300 million miles (483 million kilometers) away by cooperating radio telescopes around the world.

SCHOOL REFORM

In the spring of 1984 the Supreme Soviet approved a major reorganization of the nation's primary and secondary school system. The planned reform followed a lengthy debate about what should be done to change the educational system in the USSR. Perhaps as many as 120 million people participated in the discussion.

The changes in the school program provided for an increase in the amount of general schooling from ten to eleven years. Children now start formal education at age six instead of age seven.

The reform stressed the development of greater practical and technical skills. Many more students in their last two years of secondary schooling are guided into vocational programs. All textbooks and courses were to be reviewed and brought up to date.

FOREIGN AFFAIRS

By admission of Soviet and United States officials, the policy of detente, which is a relaxing of strained relations between nations, was allowed to lapse. By the spring of 1985 relations between the two superpowers was at the lowest level since the Cuban missile crisis in 1968. Each country blamed the other for the difficulty.

A number of events that took place contributed to the ill

feelings and unfriendly attitude displayed by each side. The United States protested the shooting down of a South Korean airliner by a Soviet fighter in September, 1983 over the Pacific Ocean resulting in the loss of 269 lives. The Soviet Union claimed that the passenger plane was involved in spying and that its air space close to the Kamchatka Peninsula was violated.

In May of 1984 the USSR withdrew from the summer Olympic games in Los Angeles, retaliating for the American withdrawal from the 1980 games in Moscow.

The Soviets continued to deploy more than 100 thousand troops in Afghanistan, occupying more towns in their war against Islamic guerrillas in the countryside.

Both the United States and the Soviet Union saw each other at fault in causing unrest and rebel warfare in Central American countries.

The greatest cause of tension and mistrust between the Soviet Union and the United States was the matter of the arms race and lack of agreement as to how to bring about disarmament. The Soviets were particularly insecure about the United States and its Western European allies positioning offensive nuclear missiles on the European continent. They were also greatly concerned over the United States research into the ability to develop space arms in order to conduct "star wars" from outer space. The United States, on the other hand, was disturbed with the Soviet Union's continuing military policy of building up its arsenal of nuclear warheads.

On the positive side of the controversy between the two opposing countries is the fact that normal diplomatic relations are being carried on and that both are participating in arms control talks from time to time in Geneva, Switzerland and elsewhere.

Right: In spring 1985, Mikhail Gorbachev's granddaughter and wife accompanied him to the polling place.
Below: General Secretary Gorbachev pays a visit to a school and talks with the students.

MIKHAIL GORBACHEV BECOMES TOP SOVIET LEADER

Upon the death of Konstantin Chernenko on March 10, 1985, Mikhail Sergeyevich Gorbachev at age fifty-four was chosen as general secretary of the Soviet Union. He thus became the most powerful leader in the USSR, and the youngest man to assume that position since Joseph Stalin assumed it in 1924 at the age of forty-five.

As the foremost figure in the Communist party and Soviet state, Gorbachev is recognized for his initiative, energy, and dedication. He is respected by Soviet citizens for his knowledgeable background in domestic and foreign affairs and for his vast experience and organizing talent.

Shortly after taking power Gorbachev stressed that the country's most important goal was rapid economic improvement. Displaying unusual impatience with its slow rate of growth, he set out to energize people by visiting factories, research institutes, and enterprises. He talked to the people outside the Kremlin with his wife, Raisa, at his side—an unprecedented practice for a modern Soviet leader. He held informal unscheduled sidewalk chats with surprised citizens of Moscow, Leningrad, and Kiev. He listened to their questions and ideas. He encouraged workers to undo bottlenecks and find ways to introduce new technology in order to increase productivity.

The USSR, the largest country in the world, has experienced tremendous growth since the revolution of 1917. Now the USSR is the most powerful Communist country in the world. With Gorbachev as its leader, the Soviet Union hopes communism will spread throughout the world and is working toward that goal through political, technological, and economic means.

Map Key
(Use the black numbers at the Arctic Circle)

Abakan	12D	Kalinin	6D	Nizhneudinsk	12D	Tambov	7D
Achinsk	12D	Kaliningrad	5D	Nizhniy-Tagil	9D	Tara	10D
Aksenovo-Zilovskoye	14D	Kaluga	6D	Noginsk	6D	Tartu	5D
Aktyubinsk	8D	Kamchatka	19D	Nordvik	14B	Tashkent	9E
Aldan	15D	Kamen-na-Obi	11D	Norilsk	11C	Taskan	18C
Aleysk	11D	Kamensk-Uralskiy	9D	Novaya Lyalya	9D	Tavda	9D
Alma-Ata	10E	Kandalaksha	6C	Novgorod	6D	Tayshet	12D
Ambarchik	19C	Kansk	12D	Novo-Kazalinsk	9E	Tbilisi	7E
Amderma	9C	Kara	9C	Novokuznetsk	11D	Termez	9F
Amga	16C	Karaga	19D	Novomoskovsk	6D	Tigil	18D
Anadyr	20C	Karaganda	10E	Novorossiysk	6E	Tikhvin	6D
Andizhan	10E	Kargasok	11D	Novosibirsk	11D	Tiksi	15B
Anzhero-Sudzhensk	11D	Karkaralinsk	10E	Novyy Port	10C	Tobolsk	9D
Aprelsk	14D	Karsakpay	9E	Nyandoma	7C	Tommot	15D
Arkhangelsk	7C	Karshi	9F	Obluchye	16E	Tomsk	11D
Armavir	7E	Kartaly	9D	Odessa	6E	Troitsk	9D
Artem	16E	Kaunas	5D	Okhotsk	17D	Tselinograd	10D
Asbest	9D	Kavacha	19C	Olekminsk	15C	Tula	6D
Ashkhabad	8F	Kazan	7D	Omsk	10D	Tulun	13D
Astrakhan	7E	Kemerovo	11D	Onega	6C	Tura	13C
Atbasar	9D	Kerch	6E	Ordzhonikidze	7E	Turgay	9E
Ayan	16D	Kezhma	13D	Orel	6D	Turkestan	9E
Baku	7E	Khabarovsk	16E	Orenburg	8D	Turtkul	9E
Balkhash	10E	Kharkov	6D	Orsk	8D	Turukhansk	11C
Barabinsk	10D	Khatanga	13B	Osh	10E	Tyndinskiy	15D
Barguzin	13D	Khilok	14D	Oymyakon	17C	Tyumen	9D
Barnaul	11D	Khorog	10F	Palana	18D	Uelen	21C
Batamav	15C	Kiev	6D	Panfilov	10E	Uelkal	21C
Batumi	7E	Kirensk	13D	Partizansk	16E	Ufa	8D
Belogorsk	15D	Kirov	7D	Pavlodar	10D	Uka	19D
Belomorsk	6C	Kirovabad	7E	Pechenga	6C	Ukhta	8C
Beloretsk	8D	Kirovsk	6C	Penza	7D	Ulyanovsk	7D
Berdichev	5E	Kishinev	6E	Perm	8D	Ulan-Ude	13D
Berezniki	8D	Kokand	10E	Petropavlovsk	9D	Uralsk	8D
Berezovo	9C	Kokchetav	9D	Petropavlovsk	18D	Urusha	15D
Birobidzhan	16E	Kolomna	6D	Petrovsk-Zabaykalskiy	13D	Usolye-Sibirskoye	13D
Biysk	11D	Komsomolsk	16D	Petrozavodsk	6C	Ussuriysk	16E
Blagoveshchensk	15D	Kostroma	7D	Plesetsk	7C	Ust-Bolsheretsk	18D
Bodaybo	14D	Krasnodar	6E	Poltava	6E	Ust-Kamchatsk	19D
Borisoglebsk	7D	Krasnovodsk	8E	Prokopyevsk	11D	Ust-Kamenogorsk	11E
Borovichi	6D	Krasnoyarsk	12D	Pskov	5D	Ust-Kut	13D
Bratsk	13D	Kurgan	9D	Pushkin	6D	Ust-Maya	16C
Brest	5D	Kursk	6D	Riga	5D	Ust-Olenek	14B
Bryansk	6D	Kustanay	9D	Rostov	6E	Ust-Srednikan	18C
Bukhara	9F	Kuybyshev	8D	Ryazan	6D	Ust-Tsilma	8C
Bulun	15B	Kuznetskiy	12D	Rybinsk	6D	Ust-Usa	8C
Chardzhou	9F	Kyakhta	13D	Salekhard	9C	Velikiy Ustyus	7C
Chelkar	8E	Kyzyl	12D	Samarkand	9F	Velsk	7C
Chelyabinsk	9D	Leninabad	9E	Saratov	7D	Verkhne-Kolymsk	18C
Cheremkhovo	13D	Leningrad	6D	Satka	8D	Verkhoyansk	16C
Chernovtsy	5E	Leninogorsk	11D	Semipalatinsk	11D	Vilnius	5D
Chimbay	8E	Leninsk-Kuznetskiy	11D	Serov	9D	Vilyuysk	15C,
Chimkent	9E	Lenkoran	7F	Serpukhov	6D	Vinnitsa	5E
Chita	14D	Lipetsk	6D	Sevastopol	6E	Vitebsk	6D
Chumikan	16D	Lvov	5E	Seymchan	18C	Vitim	14D
Dalnerechensk	16E	Lysva	8D	Shevchenko	8E	Vladivostok	16E
Darasun	14D	Magadan	18D	Shilka	14D	Volgograd	7E
Dikson	11B	Magnitogorsk	8D	Shimanovsk	15D	Vologda	6D
Dnepropetrovsk	6E	Makat	8E	Simferopol	6E	Vorkuta	9C
Donetsk	6E	Makeyevka	6E	Slavgorod	10D	Voronezh	6D
Dudinka	11C	Makhachkala	7E	Slyudyanka	13D	Voroshilovgrad	6E
Dzerzhinsk	7D	Margelan	10E	Skovorodino	15D	Vyborg	5C
Dzhambul	10E	Markovao	20C	Smolensk	6D	Vytegra	6C
Ekimchan	16D	Markovo	11C	Solikamsk	8D	Yakutsk	15C
Frunze	10E	Mary	9F	Solovyevsk	15D	Yamsk	18D
Gizhiga	19C	Medvezhyegorsk	6C	Sovetskaya Gavan	17E	Yaroslavl	6D
Golchikha	11B	Mezen	7C	Spassk-Dalniy	16E	Yelanskoye	15C
Gomel	6D	Minsk	5D	Sredne-Kolymsk	18C	Yelets	6D
Gorki	7D	Minusinsk	12D	Stavropol	7E	Yerevan	7E
Gorno-Altaysk	11D	Mogilev	6D	Sterlitamak	8D	Yessey	13C
Groznyy	7E	Mogocha	14D	Strelka	13C	Zaporozhye	6E
Guryev	8E	Moscow	6D	Sumy	6D	Zavitaya	15D
Igarka	11C	Murmansk	6C	Suntar	14C	Zaysan	11E
Irkutsk	13D	Namangan	10E	Surgut	10C	Zeya	15D
Ishim	9D	Naryan Mar	8C	Sverdlovsk	9D	Zhdanov	6E
Ivanovo	7D	Nerchinsk	14D	Svobodnyy	15D	Zhigansk	15C
Izhevsk	8D	Nikolayev	6E	Syktyvkar	8C	Zhitomir	5D
Kachuga	13D	Nizhne-Kolymsk	19C	Syzran	7D	Zlatoust	8D
				Tallinn	5D	Zima	13D

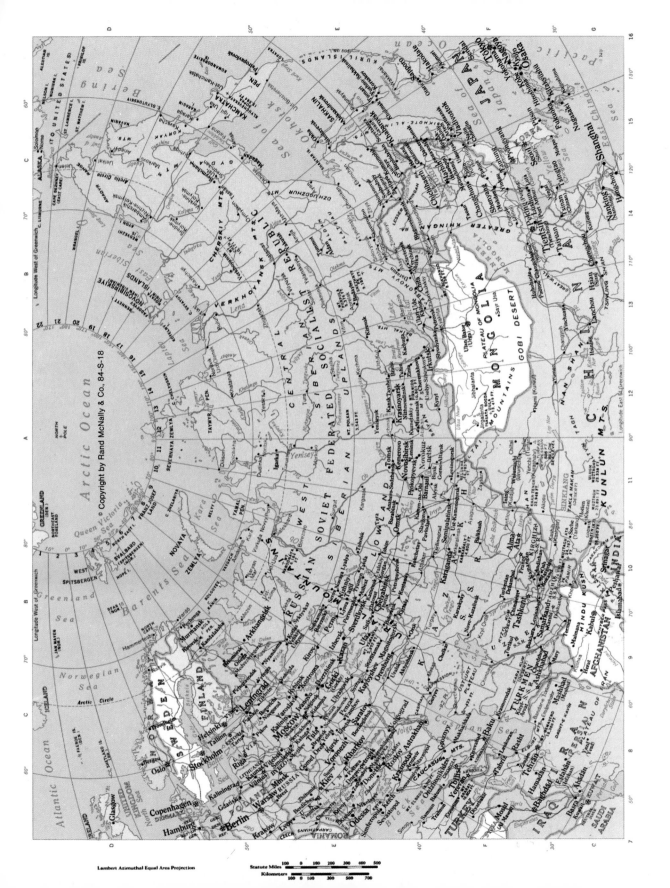

Lambert Azimuthal Equal Area Projection

Statute Miles

Kilometers

MINI-FACTS AT A GLANCE

GENERAL INFORMATION

Official Name: Union of Soviet Socialist Republics

Capital: Moscow

Official Language: Russian

Other Languages: Altaic, other Indo-European languages, Uralic, and Caucasian, among others. There are about 130 languages spoken in the Soviet Union.

Government: The Soviet Union is a federal state made up of fifteen union republics. Within some union republics there are autonomous regions and autonomous republics. The Russian Soviet Federated Socialist Republic also has ten national areas. The Soviet Union has a two-house legislature called the Supreme Soviet that includes the Soviet (Council) of the Union and the Soviet of Nationalities. Both houses carry equal weight. The members are elected for five-year terms. All citizens are allowed to vote; however, there is only one party and one candidate to vote for within that party, the Communist party. The Presidium of the Supreme Soviet, which is elected by the members of the two houses, is made up of thirty-nine members. This body acts as the head of state. It is led by a chairman. The Supreme Soviet also appoints the Council of Ministers, headed by a chairman, to establish the executive and administrative branch of government.

The Communist party has full control of the government, even though only 6 percent of all Soviet citizens belong to it. The All-Union Party Congress has about five thousand delegates from the fifteen republics of the Soviet Union, the autonomous republics, regional areas, and representatives from Communist parties all over the world. The Congress is supposed to meet every five years. Its four-hundred-member Central Committee meets at least twice a year. A Politburo (Political Bureau) and a Secretariat, selected by party leaders, are formed to act for the party during periods the All-Union Party Congress does not meet. The Politburo is the real center of power in the party and therefore the government.

The Secretariat, headed by a ten-member group of the Central Committee, makes certain that party policies are carried out. The general secretary of the Central Committee is in charge of the Secretariat and the Politburo. It is the most powerful position in the Soviet Union.

Each union republic has a constitution and a government patterned after the national government, except that republic supreme soviets have only one house. The republic councils of ministers take care of internal affairs.

National Song: *"Gosudarstveyi Gimn Sovetskogo Soyusa"* ("National Anthem of the Soviet Union")

Flag: The flag is red with a gold hammer and sickle in the upper-left corner. A five-point, fold-edged red star is above the hammer and sickle. The red stands for revolution, the hammer and sickle for united workers and peasants, and the star stands for the Communist party.

Religion: Although atheism is officially encouraged by the state, many Russians still relate to the Russian Orthodox church. Other religious groups in the country include Muslims, Buddhists; Evangelical Christian Baptists, Lutherans, Roman Catholics, Jews, Old Believers, and the Armenian Church.

Money: The basic unit of money in the Soviet Union is the ruble. One hundred kopecks equal one ruble. There are coins worth 1, 2, 3, 5, 10, 15, 20, and 50 kopecks, and also a coin worth one ruble. There are paper notes worth 1, 3, 5, 10, 25, 50, and 100 rubles. As of January 1989, one ruble equaled $1.61 in United States currency.

Weights and Measures: The Soviet Union uses the metric system.

Population: 287,800,000 (1990 estimate)

Cities:	1989 Census	1990 Estimate
Moscow (capital)	8,739,000	8,769,000
Leningrad	4,902,000	4,456,000
Kiev	2,486,000	2,587,000
Tashkent	2,076,000	2,073,000
Kharkov	1,572,000	1,611,000
Gorki	1,406,000	1,438,000
Minsk	1,503,000	1,589,000

GEOGRAPHY

Highest Point: Communism Peak, 24,590 ft. (7,495 m), found in the Pamirs.

Lowest Point: Karagiye Depression, 433 ft. (132 m) below sea level

Coastline: 30,787 mi. (49,547 km)

Greatest Distances: East to west—6,000 mi. (9,656 km)
North to south—3,200 mi. (5,150 km)

Rivers: The longest river that flows entirely within Russia is the Lena, 2,734 mi. (4,400 km) in Siberia. Other long rivers include the Amur, Ob, and Yenisay. The Volga, the longest river in Europe, is 2,194 mi. (3,531 km) long.

Lakes: The Caspian Sea, the world's largest inland body of water and a salt lake, is the largest lake. It covers 143,630 sq. mi. (372,000 km²). The deepest lake in the world is also in Russia. It is Lake Baikal in Siberia, which is 5,315 ft. (1,620 m) deep.

Mountains: Russia has a number of mountain ranges including the Carpathians, the mountains of the Caucasus and the Crimea, the Urals, and the Pamirs.

Climate: Because Russia is so vast, its climate varies considerably. It stretches from the Arctic Ocean in the north to desert lowland zones in the south. The climate is also influenced by features of the land itself, such as in the Crimea where mountains block cold air from the north. The only kinds of climate that Russia does not have are tropical forests and savannas.

The climate of Russia is continental—its summer and winter temperatures vary greatly. In Moscow, for example, the mean January temperature is 54° F. (12° C) lower than that of July. In central Germany, there is a difference of 34° F. (1° C). The degree of continentality increases going eastward. In Yakutia, in eastern Siberia, for example, the difference between the averages of the warmest and coldest months can be 108 to 117° F. (42° to 47° C).

The winters are very cold except in the Crimea. In western Siberia the snow stays on the ground for 140 to 260 days or more. The lowest temperature ever recorded on earth was recorded at Oymyakon in Siberia; it was -96° F. (-71° C). The Arctic, which does not see daylight in winter, is less cold, but more uncomfortable because of high winds.

The amount of precipitation varies in Russia from the Kara-Kum and Kyzyl-Kum deserts, where there is practically no snow cover, to West Transcaucasia where annual precipitation is greater than 80 in. (203 c) per year. On the mountain slopes of this region, the precipitation is as high as 160 in. (406 c).

Area: 8,649,500 sq. mi. (22,402,000 km²)

NATURE

Trees: There are many forests in the plains and the mountains of Russia, many with similar varieties of deciduous and evergreen trees. In the Russian plain: spruce, fir, Siberian spruce, oak, birch, beech, and linden. In the Caucasus: pine, spruce, fir, oak, hornbeam ash, beech, and wild fruit trees. In the desert lowland zone of the Causasus: laurel, palm, bamboo, and boxtree. In the western Siberian plain: spruce, cedar, pine, and fir. In central Siberia: pine forests cover about 60 percent of the area. In northeastern Siberia: larch. In the Far East: stony birch, Dahurian larch, Sayan spruce, oak, hornbeam ash, Korean cedar, maple, Manchurian nut, and fir.

Fish, ocean: Siberian salmon, humpback (Pacific salmon), herring, cod, and smelt

Fish, inland: Carp, bream, pike, perch, and vendace

Animals: In the Arctic zone: white bear, sea hare, seal, walrus, and eiders. In the tundra: polar fox, northern reindeer, white hare, and lemming. In the European-Siberian forest area: elk, brown bear, reindeer, lynx, sable, white hare, reptiles and amphibians, boar, deer, and mink. In the steppes: marmot, jerboa, Tartar fox, and the steppe polecat. In the Mediterranean subregion: the mountain goat, chamois, bezoar goat, porcupine, leopard, hyena, and jackal. In the central Asian subregion: djeiran antelope, sand cat, sand eel, earless marmot, mountain goat, snow leopard, and red wolf.

Birds: In the Arctic: sea gulls and loons. In the tundra: white partridge and polar owl; geese, swans, and ducks in the summer. In the European-Siberian forest area: crossbill, nutcracker, cuckoo, owl, and woodpecker. In the steppes: kestrel, crane, eagle, and lark. In the Mediterranean subregion: Caucasian black grouse, turkey hen, stone partridge, nuthatch, and black woodpecker. In the central Asian subregion: drofa, pheasant, and desert raven.

EVERYDAY LIFE

Food: There is a great variety of food in the Soviet Union. In the southern republics the food is similar to that found in Turkey or Greece. Lamb pieces, kebobs (*shashlyk*), and sausages on skewers cooked over an open fire are very popular, particularly in Georgia. In Siberia, where a lot of canned fish and horse and reindeer meat is eaten, there may also be some Oriental-style flavorings. In central Asia, *plov,* a mutton and rice mixture, is popular.

In the Russian parts of the USSR, lunch is the biggest meal of the day and is often eaten at work or school. Common lunch and supper foods include herring, cabbage soup, beet soup (*borscht*) fish soup (*rassolnik*), kasha (a cereal grain), cabbage, cucumbers, thin pancakes (*bliny*), and sweet Ukrainian dumplings filled with fruit (*varenyky*) served with sour cream. Russians also enjoy a type of ravioli called (*pelmeni*) and a flat dough rolled over cottage cheese served with jam, known as *syrniki.* Their *pirozhkis* are fried or baked rolls filled with meat or cabbage. Vegetables are eaten mostly in soup.

Housing: The amount of space that each person has to live in in the Soviet Union is dictated by the state. In most cases, that area is only 97 sq. ft. (9 m^2), although in the cities some of the newer apartments are larger. In Siberia, and other inhospitable climates, living space increases. This allotment is part of a plan by the government to entice people to live there.

In villages, especially in Russia and Siberia, the homes are made of wood. The windows of village houses are often quite decorative and interesting. They are enclosed by hand-carved frames usually painted blue. In the small, fenced-in backyard gardens of these country homes the villagers plant vegetables, grapevines, and sunflowers. Nearby, there is usually a cow grazing next to family-owned chickens, geese, and ducks.

In rural areas, living standards are lower than in cities. Homes often have no gas, running water, or plumbing.

Holidays (National):

> January 1, New Year's Day
> February 23, Soviet Army Day
> March 8, International Women's Day
> May 1-2, May Day
> May 9, Victory Day
> October 7, Constitution Day
> November 7-8, October Revolution

Culture: The Soviet people are heirs to a great literary tradition. Yet the written word has always been subject to censorship by the government. In spite of this hardship, great works have been written under the Soviet regime. World War I inspired much Soviet literature in the last sixty years, as did the Russian Revolution and the civil war.

Poetry recitals are very popular in the Soviet Union. Poetry Day is celebrated in December of each year. In the postrevolutionary years poetry held a special place. Vladimir Mayakovsky was one of the most revered poets of this period.

Drama has long been important in Russian literature. After the revolution Communist messages were predominant. Plays about the war followed. More recently, there has been more variety in the themes used.

The film classic *Battleship Potemkin* made by Sergei Eisenstein in 1925 is considered by many to be one of the best films ever made. Now, filmmaking has become very important in the Soviet Union. More than three hundred full-length films are produced each year. Every day eleven to twelve million people all over the country go to see films.

Music has had a rich tradition in Russia and later the Soviet Union. There are 150 philharmonic societies and over 700 symphony orchestras.

Sports and Recreation: The development of the body is so important in the USSR that it is actually encouraged in the constitution. More than 220,000 sports clubs and societies are organized around the country. Any citizen can join a sports club by paying only thirty kopecks a year and another thirty kopecks every time the facility is used. That is about the price of a movie ticket.

A variety of sports are popular in the Soviet Union. Ice hockey, soccer, basketball, and track and field are the most popular. Popular noncompetitive sports include cross-country skiing, skating, fishing, and hunting. The Soviets love to play chess. Gymnastics and wrestling are beginning to receive attention.

Communications: The press in the Soviet Union is controlled by the government, but publications are owned and published by various organizations, including the Communist party, trade unions, and cultural institutions. *Pravda,* the largest newspaper in the Soviet Union, is printed in forty-four cities.

There are about 8,000 newspapers (including 640 dailies) published in fifty-five languages spoken in the country and nine foreign languages. The most important daily in the country, *Pravda,* is controlled by the Central Committee of the Communist party.

Radio Moscow broadcasts in sixty-eight languages. Each region has its own special broadcasts as well as broadcasts for the whole country. TV can be seen in most parts of the country. There are six central TV channels and over four hundred television stations in the country.

Transportation: Historically, transporting people and goods in a country as large as Russia has not been easy; yet a number of obstacles have been overcome. Railways and pipelines are very important in the Soviet Union because road building is complicated by the harsh climate.

The USSR has one tenth of the world's railway tracks, but it accounts for more than half of the world's total rail freight traffic. In 1982, the total length of track in the Soviet Union was about 88,750 mi. (142,800 km).

Aeroflot, the national airline of the USSR, is the largest government-owned airline in the world. It flies to around eighty countries and carries about 25 percent of all the world's air passengers on some of the newest and most advanced aircraft.

Education: In the Soviet Union children begin school at age six and usually continue until age seventeen. Often school comes after two or more years spent in one of the 127,100 state-run nursery schools and kindergartens. The schools emphasize science and foreign languages, and there is much political indoctrination. Although textbooks may be written in as many as fifty-two languages, the basic curriculum is rather standard. It is designed by the ministries of education in each republic as well as the national Ministry of Education.

There are many vocational schools. Usually students enter these after seven or eight years of general school. At present, students attending vocational schools do not study the same curriculum as those who go to general secondary schools. The latter are eligible to apply to institutions of higher learning, either a university or a specialized institute. It is relatively difficult to get into these schools, however. Not only must a student have good academic records and excellent test scores, but he or she must have the "right" political and ethnic background. Jews, for example, no matter how good they are academically, have a very hard time being admitted to these schools. Tuition is free.

Health: Most health care is free in the Soviet Union. Hospitals and clinics give free service. There are over a million doctors in the country, or about thirty-eight for every ten thousand patients. So-called holiday homes and sanitoria (mostly for patients who have tuberculosis) are available in addition to hospitals and clinics. Special clinics are set up for children up to the age of sixteen.

Principal Products:

Agriculture: Barley, beef and dairy cattle, corn, cotton, flax, milk, oats, potatoes, rye, sheep, sugar beets, tobacco, vegetables, wheat, wool
Manufacturing: Chemicals, electrical and electronic equipment, iron and steel, lumber, machinery, paper, petroleum products, processed foods, processed metals, textiles, transportation equipment

IMPORTANT PEOPLE

Yuri Andropov (1914-84), general secretary of the Communist party from 1982 to 1984

Isaak Babel (1894-1941), writer

Pavel Belyayev (1925-70), cosmonaut

Aleksandr Benois (1870-1960), painter, scenic and costume designer

Lavrenty Beria (1899-1953), politician and chief of secret police

Leonid Brezhnev (1906-82), head of Communist party, 1964-82

Boris Bugaev, *pseudonym* Andrey Bely (1880-1934), poet and novelist

Mikhail Bulgakov (1891-1940), novelist and playwright

Nikolay Bulganin (1895-1975), premier, 1955-58

Fyodor Chaliapin (1873-1938), singer

Konstantin Chernenko (1911-1985), became general secretary of the Communist party in 1984

Georgy Dobrovolsky (1928-71), cosmonaut

Nino Efimova (1877-1948), puppeteer, invented hand-and-rod puppet

Sergei Eisenstein (1898-1948), film director

Sergei Esenin (1895-1925), poet

Aleksander Fadeyev (1901-56), novelist

Konstantin Fedin (1892-1977), novelist

Aleksandr Fersman (1883-1945), mineralogist, a founder of geochemistry

Alexander Friedmann (1888-1925), mathematician and physical scientist

Mikhail Frunze (1885-1925), army commander, one of the fathers of the Red Army

Yuri Gagarin (1934-68), cosmonaut, first man to travel in space

Aleksandr Glazunov (1865-1936), composer

Mikhail Gorbachev (1931-   ), president and general secretary of the Soviet Union

Anna Gorenko, *pseudonym* Anna Akhmatova (1889-1966), considered greatest woman poet in Russian literature

Aleksandr Grechaninov (1864-1956), composer

Andrei Gromyko (1906-   ), foreign minister of the Soviet Union from 1957 to 1985

Sergey Ilyushin (1894-1977), aircraft designer

Dmitri Kabalevsky (1903-   ), composer

Mikhail Kalinin (1875-1946), politician

Alexander Kerensky (1881-1970), premier of the first provisional government after first revolution in 1917

Aram Khachaturian (1903-78), composer

Nikita Khrushchev (1894-1971), leader of the Soviet Union, 1958-64

Aleksandra Kollontay (1872-1952), commissar and diplomat, first woman ambassador in the world

Vladimir Komarov (1927-67), cosmonaut, first man known to have died during a space mission

Ivan Konev (1897-1973), general, commander in chief of Soviet army from 1946 to 1960

Sergey Korolyov (1906-66), aeronautical engineer, director of space program

Aleksay Kosygin (1904-80), premier of the Soviet Union, 1964-80

Lenin (Vladimir Ilyich Ulyanov) (1870-1924), founder of the Bolshevik party and leader in the revolution and first Communist dictator

Osip Mandelshtam (1891-1938), poet

Vladimir Mayakovsky (1893-1930), poet and satirist

David Oistrakh (1908-74), violinist

Boris Pasternak (1890-1960), poet and novelist, won Nobel Prize in literature in 1958

Ivan Pavlov (1849-1936), physiologist, won Nobel Prize for physiology or medicine in 1904

Aleksev Peshkov, *pen name* Maxim Gorky (1868-1936), writer

Nikolai Podgorny (1903-83), chairman of the Presidium of the Supreme Soviet, 1965-77

Sergei Prokofiev (1891-1953), composer

Ilya Repin (1844-1930), painter

Svetlana Savitskaya, first woman to walk in space

Mikhail Sholokhov (1905-1984), novelist

Dmitri Shostakovich (1906-75), composer, considered greatest symphonist of the mid-twentieth century

Joseph Stalin (1879-1953), dictator of the Soviet Union from 1929 to 1953

Leon Trotsky (1879-1940), a leader of the Bolshevik revolution

Maria Tsvetaeva (1892-1941), poet

Andrey Vyshinsky (1883-1954), diplomat and politician

Yevgeni Yevtushenko (1933-   ), poet

IMPORTANT DATES

1917 — Revolution of March and November; Tsar Nicholas II abdicates

1918 — Treaty of Brest-Litovsk ends World War I on eastern front; tsar and his family murdered; beginning of Russian civil war

1919 — Lenin establishes the *Comintern* (Communist International)

1921 — End of civil war in Russia

1922 — USSR established; Stalin becomes general secretary of the Communist party

1924 — Lenin dies

1929 — First five-year plan

1932-33 — Famine in USSR

1933 — Hitler takes control in Germany

1934 — USSR joins League of Nations

1936-38 — Stalinist purges

1939 — Hitler invades Poland, beginning World War II; USSR invades Poland and Finland

1940 — Finland surrenders, gives up some territory

1941 — Germany invades USSR; beginning of siege of Leningrad

1942-43 — Battle of Stalingrad

1943 — Teheran conference of Allied leaders

1944 — End of siege of Leningrad

1945 — Conference at Yalta among Allied leaders; Germans and Japanese surrender, ending World War II

1948 — West Berlin blockaded by the Soviets

1949 — USSR establishes COMECON (Council for Mutual Economic Assistance); formation of NATO

1953 — Stalin dies; collective leadership rules the USSR; Georgi Malenkov becomes chairman of Council of Ministers; Khrushchev becomes head of the Communist party (first secretary)

1955—Malenkov forced to resign; Nikolai Bulganin becomes premier (Khrushchev retains real power)

1956—Khrushchev criticizes Stalin in a secret speech; beginning of de-Stalinization; revolt in Hungary and Poland

1957—*Sputnik I*, world's first spacecraft, put in orbit

1958—Khrushchev becomes chairman of the Council of Ministers

1961—Berlin Wall built; Yuri Gagarin becomes first man in space

1962—Cuban missile crisis

1963—USSR, USA, and Great Britain sign treaty banning nuclear weapons tests except those underground

1964—Khrushchev removed from office; Aleksei Kosygin becomes first secretary of the Communist party Central Committee

1968—Soviet troops invade Czechoslovakia

1969—Russia and China fight limited battles in border dispute

1972—USSR and USA sign treaty to limit production of nuclear weapons

1973—USA and USSR sign an arms limitation agreement

1977—Leonid Brezhnev becomes chairman of the Presidium of the Supreme Soviet

1979—USSR and USA sign the Strategic Arms Limitation Treaty (SALT II); ratification by the U.S. government delayed in protest over invasion of Afghanistan

1980—Kosygin retires and is replaced by Nikolai Tikhonov; Olympic games held in Moscow, boycotted by the USA

1982—Leonid Brezhnev dies, succeeded by Yuri V. Andropov

1984—Yuri Andropov dies, succeeded by Konstantin Chernenko; USSR declined to participate in the Olympic games held in Los Angeles, California

1985—Konstantin Chernenko dies, succeeded by Mikhail Gorbachev

1988—Mikhail Gorbachev takes on the title of president as well as general secretary and uses his increased power to begin a policy of *glasnost*, or *openness to new ways*

1989—The USSR holds popular elections for some government posts; more freedom of speech is permitted than ever before under the communist government

1990—The Central Committee approved a draft platform that will, in effect, end the Communist party's monopoly on political and economic life

INDEX

Page numbers that appear in boldface type indicate illustrations

About the Author

Abraham Resnick, a native New Jerseyan, is a noted author and educator specializing in elementary and secondary social studies education. As a teacher of teachers Dr. Resnick has had an outstanding career as a professor, writer, supervisor, consultant, and professional leader in the social sciences. His writings include text and trade books for children, teachers' editions of school materials, published resource units, map transparencies, and professional books and articles. He is the author of another Enchantment of the World title; *Russia: A History to 1917.*

The author enlisted in the armed forces during World War II, serving as a weatherman in the United States Army Air Corps.

Dr. Resnick's graduate work was completed at Teachers College, Columbia University in New York and Rutgers—The State University of New Jersey. He has received two writing awards from the National Council for Geographic Education as well as numerous other honors. He is presently serving as Professor of Education at Jersey City State College (New Jersey) and for many years was the Director of the Instructional Materials Center, Rutgers Graduate School of Education. In 1975 he was the recipient of that school's Alumni Award for Distinguished Service to Education.

When he isn't writing or teaching Abe Resnick enjoys watching professional sporting events, playing tennis, long distance walking, bike riding, and travel to remote regions of the world.